I0439054

OCS Study
MMS 2005-038

Coastal Marine Institute

Characterization of Algal-Invertebrate Mats at Offshore Platforms and the Assessment of Methods for Artificial Substrate Studies

Final Report

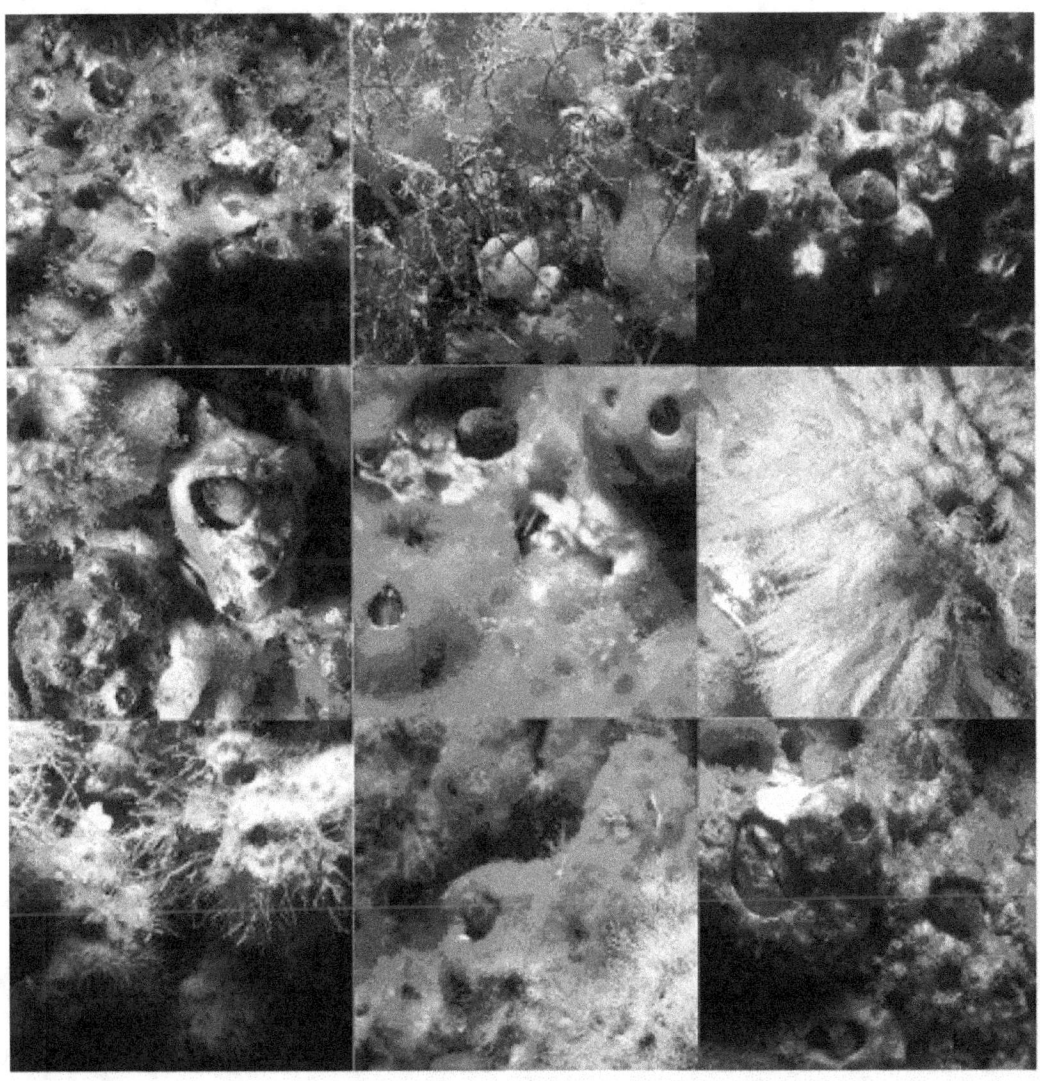

U.S. Department of the Interior
Minerals Management Service
Gulf of Mexico OCS Region

Cooperative Agreement
Coastal Marine Institute
Louisiana State University

OCS Study
MMS 2005-038

Coastal Marine Institute

Characterization of Algal-Invertebrate Mats at Offshore Platforms and the Assessment of Methods for Artificial Substrate Studies

Final Report

Author

R.S. Carney

June 2005

Prepared under MMS Contract
14-35-0001-30660-19932
by
Coastal Marine Institute
Louisiana State University
Baton Rouge, Louisiana 70803

Published by

U.S. Department of the Interior
Minerals Management Service
Gulf of Mexico OCS Region

Cooperative Agreement
Coastal Marine Institute
Louisiana State University

DISCLAIMER

This report was prepared under contract between the Minerals Management Service (MMS) and Louisiana State University. This report has been technically reviewed by the MMS and approved for publication. Approval does not signify that the contents necessarily reflect the views and policies of the Service, nor does mention of trade names or commercial products constitute endorsement or recommendation for use. It is, however, exempt from review and compliance with MMS editorial standards.

REPORT AVAILABILITY

Extra copies of the report may be obtained from the Public Information Office (Mail Stop 5034) at the following address:

U.S. Department of the Interior
Minerals Management Service
Gulf of Mexico OCS Region
Public Information Office (MS 5034)
1201 Elmwood Park Boulevard
New Orleans, Louisiana 70123-2394
Telephone Number: (504) 736-2519
1-800-200-GULF

CITATION

Suggested citation:

Carney, R.S. 2005. Characterization of Algal-Invertebrate Mats at Offshore Platforms and the Assessment of Methods for Artificial Substrate Studies: Final Report. U.S. Dept. of the Interior, Minerals Management Service, Gulf of Mexico OCS, New Orleans, La. OCS Study MMS 2005-038. 93 pp.

SUMMARY

The composition of biofouling communities on three offshore platforms in the Gulf of Mexico was examined. A platform in South Timbalier block 54 lay in 22 m of water 40 km from shore. A platform in Grand Isle block 94 lay in 60 m of water 86 km offshore. A platform in Green Canyon lease block 18 lay in 219 m at 150 km offshore near the edge of the continental shelf. The three platforms had been the site of previous fisheries-related investigations and offered an offshore gradient. Research operations were carried out from the platforms with Exxon and Mobil corporations hosting and providing logistical support. Field sampling was initiated in November 1995, and completed September 1997.

Video surveying, high-resolution photography, surface scraping, and settling plates were employed to describe the biota and to evaluate the effectiveness of the methods. Combined, the methods showed that the inshore ST-54 platform biota conformed to a previously recognized inshore type dominated by barnacles with overgrowths of algae and hydroids. The more seaward platforms conformed to a previously recognized offshore type dominated by a mix of bivalves and larger barnacles overgrown by sponges, hydroids, and ectoprocts (bryozoans). No evidence could be found of a bluewater assemblage. Settling plates showed that new crust was forming at a slower rate at the most offshore platform, GC-18.

A scenario was developed which viewed the biofouling crust as a system in equilibrium between accretionary growth and crust shedding. Loss of crust is a direct consequence of the vertical orientation of platform benthos and is an important factor distinguishing platforms from natural systems. Accretion of the crust is dependent on the passing ocean water for food and new larval settlement. Biotic interactions such as predation, competition, and bioerosion all contribute to crust loss directly or in concert with wave surge. The ecological scenario of an equilibrium system helps identify high priority research questions.

Of the methods applied, all provided data and some degree of understanding. Video survey, however, proved a poor tool for obtaining quantitative data on species composition, but was very useful for planning and site characterization. The higher resolution of photography was better for quantitative data, the complexity of layered assemblages escaped documentation. Scrape samples were most informative but lacked consistent quantification. Settling plates produced important rate information, but the demands on dive time proved unrealistic given constraints of weather and conflicting platform operations.

ACKNOWLEDGMENTS

This project required the cooperation and assistance of many people. The Coastal Marine Institute program of Minerals Management Service provided funding. Exxon-Mobil provided helicopter transportation, vessel shipping, and platform accommodations. Drs. Chuck Wilson and David Stanley arranged this industry cooperation. Dr. Stanley oversaw multiple platform projects. Dr. James Tolan directed diving. The diving party included J. Tolan, D. Stanley, Mark Miller, Ann Bull, Alan Roy, Joel Chaky, and Frank Shaughnessy. Dr. Shaughnessy initiated algal studies while in the laboratory of Dr. Russ Chapman. Elaine Evers, Debra Waters, and Floyd Demers provided technical support. Converting images and samples to data was largely carried out by undergraduate student workers: Kevin Kasovitch, Hal Palmer, Robin Hawes, Amanda Appelbaum, Lisa Appelbaum, Jonathan Comish, and Dmetry Chuenko. Dr. Mary Boatman of MMS contributed greatly to the improvement and completion of project reporting.

TABLE OF CONTENTS

FIGURES

TABLES

1   INTRODUCTION

1.1   A UNIQUE PLACE AND TIME

The "oil patch" of the northwest Gulf of Mexico is a unique marine system in several regards; possibly the most ecologically important aspect is the extent of introduced structure. From the late 1940's to the present, oil and gas production has resulted in the installation of thousands of hard substrate islands from Mobile Bay westward and from coastal embayment to beyond the edge of the continental shelf. While it is possible to view this construction as an extension of natural hard bottom, it may be ecologically accurate to consider it a whole new habitat, a steel archipelago. It extends from bottom through the euphotic, tidal, and wave splash zones. Unlike natural seafloor hardgrounds, which can accrete shells and tests into bioherms, the predominantly vertical surfaces of platforms shed these same building components due to waves, predation, and gravity. As a result, the dynamics of platform biota are unlike natural systems.

This manmade system is now at a unique time in its development. The number and area of bottom-to-surface platform habitats in the Gulf of Mexico is probably near or at maximum right now (A. Pulsipher per. comm.). Many, if not most, new wells in deep water will employ subsea technologies, and inshore development will make more efficient use of smaller structures. Older structures will be removed, and even if large numbers are cut or toppled to create fish habitat, the most productive upper zone will be lost. From now on, the unique platform ecosystem is likely to be in decline.

The study reported herein was undertaken with two purposes. First on a shorter term, the encrusting biota of three platforms west of the Mississippi River were surveyed to compliment extensive fish studies at those same locations. Second with longer-term intent, the methods and logistics of platform surveying were being tested with respect to additional investigation. Certain aspects of platform ecology have been examined in a series of studies; mostly for fish and least for smaller biota (Beaver et al. 2003; Bedinger and Kirby 1981; Bull and Kendall 1994; Bert and Humm 1979; Dokken et al 2000; Fotheringham 1981; Gallaway et al 1981a, 1981b; George and Thomas 1979; Gunter and Geyer 1955; Keenan et al. 2003; Middleditch 1981; Stanley and Scarborough-Bull 2003; Stanley and Wilson 1997; Tolan 2001). Limited observations have been generalized to characterize the larger region; most notably Gallaway and Lewbel (1982). Much fundamental information remains to be found, however, and the validity of previous generalizations requires examination.

1.2   A HISTORY OF APPROACHES TO MARINE FOULING COMMUNITIES

This brief review traces the questions that have driven the larger study of biofouling research since the 1950's. Most work has been undertaken for practical reasons of vessel operation and structure deterioration. Although seemingly ideal systems for application of ecological theory, few such investigations can be found. Where ecological investigation has taken place, fundamental parameters such as primary and secondary production remain to be effectively measured due to difficulties of methodology.

1.2.1   Starting with Drag and Deterioration Questions

As with many ocean phenomena that impacted wartime naval operations, biological fouling of ships, buoys, and other manmade structures in the marine environment underwent close scrutiny during World War II. Biological films thinner than a millimeter were known to increase drag, and fouling was implicated as an agent in destructive corrosion. Studies carried out during the war years by a multi-investigator team at Woods Hole Oceanographic Institution produced a seminal monograph Marine Fouling and It's Prevention (Woods Hole Oceanographic Institution, 1952). The research included biotic surveys in all US coastal waters and experimental fouling-plate studies at the University of Miami.

Although the purpose of the Navy-funded work at Woods Hole/Miami was primarily engineering, those studies established an ecological perspective of fouling communities that is still prevalent. Notably, fouling organisms should be studied as a community. Such fouling communities, lack strong internal controls, show little true succession beyond an initial microbial film stage, and are strongly influenced by seasonal larval availability. In more contemporary terms, the species structure of biofouling communities is less controlled by the dynamics of the community, and more controlled by the supply of competent larvae in the region. The studies considered the Gulf of Mexico as transitional between temperate and tropical Atlantic regions.

By the time of publication of the Woods Hole/Miami studies, the use of paints containing the biocide tributyltin was proving an effective means of fouling control. This ushered in two decades of biofouling research focusing almost exclusively on antifouling. Some researchers, like Pequegnat (Pequegnat and Pequegnat 1968) managed to incorporate ecological observations in antifoulant testing, but community studies were otherwise rare. By the 1970s, self-polishing tributyltin paints had been perfected as a controlled-release toxic means of reducing fouling for five or more years. Success of these paints caused a decline in biofouling studies until tributyltin usage was severely restricted in the 1980s due to pollution concerns (Evans 1999). Efforts to find acceptable alternative antifouling agents presently support considerable biofouling research. Since microbial films play both promoter and inhibitor roles in fouling (Mitchell and Kirchman 1984, Maki et al. 1994), they have become the primary focus of research. This research is heavily biochemical in nature with little community ecology relevance (e.g. Steinberg et al. 2001).

1.2.2 Influenced by Community Ecology Theory

The Woods Hole/Miami studies anticipated that biofouling should be studied from a community perspective at a time when few community concepts had been formalized and quantified. There were few models available to drive definitive research until the late 1960's when MacArthur and Wilson (1967) proposed a general model for island zoogeography and MacArthur (1972) proposed a conceptual basis for the general study of distributions. Connell's work on competing barnacle populations (Connell 1961), Paine's work on regulation by predators (Paine 1974), and Dayton's work on disturbance (Dayton 1971) all showed the great utility of sessile benthic communities in experimental ecology, although none of that work examined artificial biofouling systems.

Surprisingly, few ecologists in the 60's and 70's tried to take advantage of the easy manipulation of biofouling communities for experimental purposes. Two studies are noteworthy, Schoener's use of settling plates in Puget Sound (Schoener 1974) and Sutherland's use of a similar system at Beaufort, N.C. Sutherland was specifically examining the conjecture of the Woods Hole/Miami study that fouling communities lacked community control by strong inter-species interactions (Sutherland and Karlson 1977). The well-designed experiment sought to determine the effect on final community structure exerted by the presence of dominant sessile organisms by their selective removal. No strong inter-species interactions were found. It was concluded that seasonal larval availability was a more important determination of community structure than competition for space by settled forms. Unfortunately, these experiments were never repeated in other environments, for longer periods of time, and using larger substrates.

In the past few years there has been resurgence in descriptive biofouling community studies for two reasons. First are the reef-like functions of platforms and artificial reefs (Bohnsack and Bannerot 1986, Pitcher and Seaman 2000) in the sense of supporting desirable fish populations. The second addresses the habitat function for invertebrate species of special interest in both positive and negative senses. Positively, platforms may afford a refuge habitat for endangered corals (P. Sammarco, per com.). Negatively, platforms may afford a stepping-stone habitat for invasive pests (Foster and Willan 1979).

An important conjecture that has arisen recently is that platform communities do actually experience strong biotic control arising from species interaction (Bull and Kendall 1994). If this is the case, then previous conclusions that strong interaction are missing arose incorrectly from: (1) short experimental duration, (2) use of small-scale settlement experiments, and (3) narrow taxonomic focus on sessile fauna (barnacles, mussels, bryozoa, etc.) rather than the mobile fauna (amphipods, ophiuroids, etc.) occupying the sessile matrix.

1.3 GULF OF MEXICO RESEARCH HISTORY

Early platform fouling work in the Gulf of Mexico through the late 1970's has been reviewed and the collective findings combined into an ecological synthesis by Gallaway and Lewbel (1982). Rather than repeat that work, the review presented here is intended as an update and a consideration of where Gulf work fits into the larger research picture developed above.

The Gulf of Mexico lies south of the range of shallow mytilid mussels with the important result that drag on submerged structures caused by biofouling is not a major engineering problem. As such, there has been relatively little engineering-based research undertaken and even less published. Gunter and Geyer (1955) completed the first biotic inventory of platforms using deployed metal cylinders at a time when oil and gas development was accelerating but still restricted mainly to near-shore areas. Development continued without much ecological monitoring until passage of the National Environmental Policy Act in 1969. Three resulting studies in the Gulf of Mexico included fouling communities in multi-component investigations (Ward et al. 1979; Middleditch 1981; Bedinger and Kirby 1981).

The Offshore Ecology Investigations (OEI) in Timbalier Bay, Louisiana and adjacent offshore regions overlapped the current study area (Ward et al. 1979). Most components were intended to test for effects in the environment around platforms (Carney 1987), but two addressed platform biota directly. Component studies produced a checklist of algal species (Bert and Humm 1979) and a biofouling community dynamics study (George and Thomas 1979). The algal checklist has been updated in Appendix A. Seven platforms were sampled ranging from a coastal bay to outer shelf. Algal occurrence was noted without respect to depth. The fouling community dynamics study assumed the sampled communities to be in a stable climax condition rather than a dynamic state of change.

Platform biofouling continued to be investigated in the context of pollution effects during the Buccaneer Gas and Oil Field Study off the Texas coast (partially presented in Middleditch 1981). Biofouling was studied in a survey context (Fotheringham 1981), and as a subcomponent in a systems-ecology approach (Gallaway et al. 1981a). A final whole-system model (Fucik and Show 1981) simulated biomass and carbon flux, but not community structure with the fouling component.

The Central Gulf Platform Study (Bedinger and Kirby 1981) was a comprehensive effects study conducted off Louisiana. It included a biofouling component (Gallaway et al. 1981b). The results from the Buccaneer Gas and Oil Field Study, the Central Gulf Study, and previous results were combined into an overall synthesis (Gallaway and Lewbel 1982) that remains a definitive today. Of particular importance are the models produced by these studies, which provide a guide to future studies that move to smaller scales to examine inner functions of the biofouling community and also move to larger scales to examine northern Gulf ecosystem functions.

More recently, the systems ecology approach with an emphasis on fish populations has been continued in a series of investigations by Dokken's group at Texas A&M Corpus Christi. A useful summary of results can be found in Dokken et al. (2000). Nine artificial and platform reefs lying from 11 to 194 km offshore in water depths of 30 to 260 m were surveyed for biofouling and/or fish communities between 1994 and 1997. Encrusted faunal communities were nondestructively surveyed photographically at fixed 1.5 m intervals along vertical transects. The imaged area was 0.47 m^2, and encrusted fauna was analyzed by classification and counting of 100 random points. Random scraping of 0.25 m^2 areas provided ground-truth. Analysis and synthesis were considered consistent with Gallaway and Lewbel (1982). Community structure changed inshore to offshore. As many as four vertical zones were recognized. The shallowest being influenced by wave energy and the deepest by the prevalent continental shelf turbid layer.

While most Gulf of Mexico studies have been directed at platform effects or, more recently, reef-like effects in the northwestern Gulf of Mexico, Pequegnat and Pequegnat (1968) carried out a distinctly different study in the eastern Gulf. The primary purpose of the study was evaluation of organo-tin antifoulants. It did not examine platform biofouling, but looked at introduced substrates on deployments near three "Texas Towers" (instrumented structures) located 2, 11, and 25 miles off the coast of Panama City, FL. The experimental substrates were plastic floats. Four floats were suspended from cross rungs of a ladder-like frame. The frames were suspended on a line at 4, 10, and 17 m below the surface at each of the 3 sites. The 11 and 25-mile stations had an additional array at 29 m, and the 25 mile station had an array at 44 m. Floats were deployed and harvested at intervals ranging from two weeks to a year. An especially interesting aspect of the methods used was harvesting in a manner assuring recovery of small mobile fauna. Bags were slipped over each substrate before it was cut loose, trapping all fauna. Approximately 680 substrates were analyzed yielding 187 species. The study produced three important results: (1) species settlement is closely linked to water-mass bathing the substrates, (2) hydroids and gammarid amphipods contribute to very large transient biomass pulses, (3) the fouling species are different than those found in the later studies to the west.

1.4 GULF OF MEXICO RESEARCH SYNTHESIS

The most influential biofouling studies conducted in the Gulf of Mexico, in terms of providing an overview of community structure and function, have been the biofouling studies at Buccaneer Field (Gallaway et al.1981a) and Central Gulf Platform Study (Gallaway et al 1981b) conducted by LGL Ecological Research Associates. Results were summarized in two readily available reports. These two studies along with previous work were developed into an overall synthesis (Gallaway and Lewbel 1982).

An onshore-offshore change in the biota of 20 studied platforms was recognized as reflecting a gradient of change (ecotonal) rather than internally homogenous distinct zones. Three general assemblage types were recognized on the basis of dominant fauna and indicator species. Especially obvious was a shift from dominance by barnacles inshore to pelycepods offshore.

1. Inshore—From shore to mid shelf (0-m to 30-m depth) encrusting fauna was dominated by smaller balanoid barnacles overgrown by algae (shallow) and hydroid (deeper) mats.

2. Offshore—At midshelf (30-m to 60-m depth) barnacles and pelycepods (primarily *Isognomon bicolor*) were co-dominants at the surface. Deeper, barnacles became rare and large cemented pelycepods were common (*Hyatissa thomasi* and *Chama macerophylla*). The octocoral *Telesto* sp. was considered a reliable indicator species of this assemblage.

3. Blue Water Platforms—This assemblage was considered characteristic of water depths greater than 60-m depths along the outer third of the continental shelf. It was not well characterized due to a lack of quantitative samples. Barnacles were reported as predominantly lepidaform (stalked), although balanoids were present. Pelycepods were also dominant. Shelf edge hard bottom forms such as spiny lobster *Palinurus* and urchin *Euciaris tribuloides* were common.

The more recent surveys off Texas (Dokken et al. 2000) are somewhat difficult to compare with the Gallaway-Lewbel biogeographic scheme since the former established faunal patterns from cluster analysis and the latter was a narrative assessment. In general the Texas platforms represented three biotic clusters. All three might fit within Gallaway-Lewbel offshore zone. There was not a simple offshore or depth ordering of the clusters. An obvious blue-water zone, in the sense of encountering stalked barnacles, was not encountered in spite of the considerable distance from land.

2 OBJECTIVES AND METHODS

2.1 OBJECTIVES

Three well-studied platforms were examined to obtain information about the fouling organisms and to determine optimal surveying approaches. The specific objectives of the proposed task were threefold.

1. Describe the biofouling communities at three oil platforms previously investigated during bioacoustic studies and compare with Gallaway and Lewbel's (1982) scheme of inshore-offshore gradient.

2. Evaluate the effectiveness of surveying methods in order to identify those most suitable for wider-area, longer-time studies and be capable of supporting hypothesis testing.

3. Develop high quality voucher collections at LSU and the U.S. National Museum of Natural History to facilitate taxonomic QA/QC in the future.

2.2 INITIAL DESIGN

The proposed approach was a modification of diver surveys of subtidal epibiota cover and composition (Andrew and Mapstone, 1987) involving fixed vertical /horizontal transects, stratified random scraping, and settling plate placement/recovery. Three aspects of biotic pattern were to be determined.

1. Within Platform Variation—Since platforms are structurally complex with numerous vertical members and cross braces interacting with the current field, what is the variation of the fouling community spatially?

2. Among Platform Variation—Since the location of a platform determines the oceanographic conditions experienced, what is the difference between the platforms and how does this difference compare with Gallaway and Lewbel's proposed zonation? Since it is logistically infeasible to replicate platforms within zones, platform effects will be confounded with location effects.

3. Temporal Variation—platforms experience different currents and exposure to coastal or oceanic water masses during the year, what happens to the community structure and to the composition of newly settled (with survival to collection) organisms during a year?

The original intent of the study was to visit three platforms as often as three to four times in a year. Biota would be surveyed at medium resolution by video, at high resolution with 35mm photography, ground truthed by scrape sampling, and settlement studied with settling plates. Within platform variation would be determined by sampling at fixed depth intervals (1 m, 5 m, 10 m, 20 m, and 30 m) at two separate legs on each platform. Suction sampling of mobile fauna from the biofouling crust was attempted on a trial basis, but then pursued in a separate study of fish larvae (Tolan 2001). Unfortunately, execution of the original design proved impossible due to weather cancellation of field trips, weather restrictions on diving once on platforms, and conflicts with platform operation schedules.

2.3 SITES

Three offshore production platforms were surveyed, Grand Isle 94 (GI-94), South Timbalier 54 (ST-54) and Green Canyon 18 (GC-18) (Figure 2.1). These sites were originally selected as an offshore transect for fish acoustic surveys (Stanley and Wilson 1996, 1997) and have been included in fish larval (Tolan 2001) and fish feeding studies (Keenan et al. 2003).

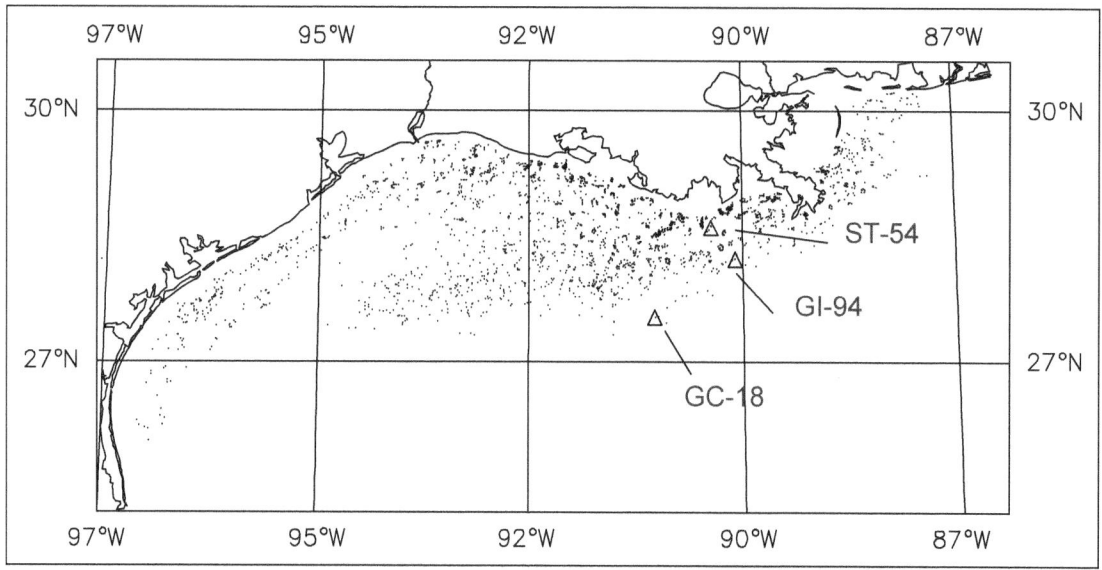

Figure 2.1. Location of study sites.

ST-54 lies in only 22 m of water at 28°50.01'N and 90°22.40'W. It was installed in 1956 and is operated by Exxon USA. It is an eight-pile production platform 40 km from the nearest land. GI-94 lies in 60 m of water at 28°31.33'N and 90°05.52'W. It was installed in 1975 and was operated by Mobil USA Inc. at the time of the study. It is an eight-pile production platform 86 km from land. GC-18 lies in 219 m at 27°56.48'N and 91°02.28'W. It was installed in 1988 and was operated by Mobil USA. It is a six-pile production platform near the edge of the continental shelf 150 km from land.

According to distance offshore and water depth (Figure 2.2), the selected platforms should lie in each of the three platform assemblage zones established by Gallaway and Lewbel (1982). ST-54 should lie in coastal assemblage zone, GI-94 in the offshore zone and GC-18 in the blue water zone. The platforms are, however, relatively close to the mouth of the Mississippi River and experience a more complex set of hydrographic conditions than anticipated by Gallaway and Lewbel zones that parallel the coast. The region enclosing the three survey platforms is subject to considerable annual and shorter-term fluctuation in salinity and temperature. Winds and river discharge cause a general cross-shelf progression of a warm lower-salinity coastal front during the spring and summer months. This front cools, retreats, breaks down, and submerges in the winter, allowing high-salinity, warmer oceanic water to encroach landward. Superimposed on this general pattern of moving coastal versus oceanic water, low-salinity threads and lenses of Mississippi discharge transit the region at all times of year.

Annual surface temperatures at all three platforms range from 20 to 30 degrees Celsius accompanied with a salinity variation of 25 to 35.5 ppt. ST-54 experiences this full range but oceanic salinities are relatively rare. GC-18 experiences the same range, but coastal salinities are much more rare. GI-94 is somewhat intermediate, but experiences conditions more similar to the seaward platform than the nearshore ST-54.

Seasonally reduced oxygen (hypoxia) and high turbidity are bottom-associated phenomena that can be expected to effect biotic colonization. Hypoxia approaching anoxia is a seasonal bottom and near-bottom condition associated with elevated river-driven production in the poorly mixed water landward of the summer coastal front (Rabalais et al. 1985). ST-54 lies in such shallow water that the platform legs below 15 m experience marked seasonal hypoxia. At 60m depth, the 0 to 30-m depth range of this study for GI-94 lies above major oxygen reduction. Similarly, the 219-m water depth at GC-18 effectively isolates the zone of study from any bottom hypoxia. High rates of fine sediment influx and bottom mixing processes give rise to a semi- permanent bottom boundary layer with a high suspended sediment load (McGrail and Carnes 1983). It is generally agreed that this turbid or nephloid layer restricts biotic colonization within more than 10 m of bottom west of the Mississippi River mouth. East of the river, a similar ecologically important turbid layer is absent or more transient. As with hypoxia, the effect on turbidity on biotic colonization is mediated by depth. The study depths at shallow ST-54 lie within the turbid layer. The study depths at GI-94 and GC-18 lie above the turbid layer.

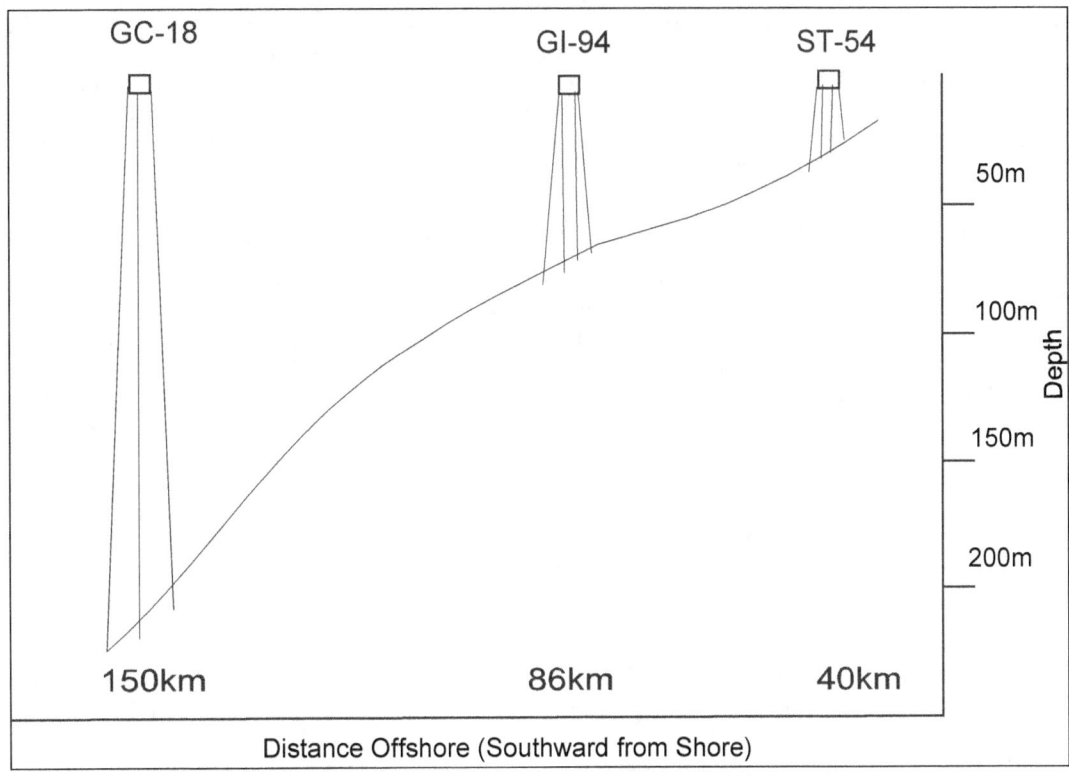

Figure 2.2. Schematic of depth and distance from shore of study platforms.

2.4   35-mm Photosurvey

Photographic surveying has been a major component of previous platform biofouling studies in the Gulf of Mexico since the OEI study. Ideally, it provides a means of rapidly recording images of multiple surface areas on a platform from which presence and percent cover data can be obtained. Paired with some actual sampling of the biofouling crust to establish species identifications, photosurvey greatly increases the area over which distribution patterns can be determined.

2.4.1   Photosurvey Methods Background

Seafloor photography did not become a practical survey tool until the development of reliable, battery-powered xenon flash in 1932 by Dr. Harold Edgerton of MIT (Edgerton 1983). Early seafloor surveys were largely qualitative (Vevers 1951, Laughton 1959). The methodology was not widely employed initially, since it was not considered adequate for assessing the soft bottom habitats. When concerns about global reef status increased dramatically in the 1970's, it was realized that reliable quantification and rigorous survey designs were badly needed (Loya 1978). Photography was quickly recognized as a quantitative tool, replacing time-consuming *in situ* diver assessment with more accurate point counting of photographic images (Bohnsack 1979). Great concern about statistical rigor in hypothesis testing lead to careful consideration of photosurvey sampling design (Dodge et al. 1982). Fortunately, equipment was inexpensive since the popularity of SCUBA diving had driven commercial development of moderately priced underwater cameras (Nikonos I in 1963) and strobes such as the Ikelite brand.

The primary methods of obtaining data from reef images is point counting, a means of estimating area with a long history in several image-based disciplines. Applied to reef studies, it has been strongly

7

influenced by point counting in petrography (Chayes 1956). The method consists of classifying and counting a number of points on an image and then equating the proportion of points in each category (species) to image area covered. Determining the optimal (effort versus accuracy) number of points to count is still an unresolved problem, although geological and ecological applications frequently make use of van der Plas and Tobi's (1965) table to assess adequacy. There used to be a debate as to the best placement of points. Randomly scattered points were statistically preferable, but time-consuming to generate when many images needed to be analyzed. Fixed grids were easy to generate, but might impose bias if the underlying patterns were linear. Today, with computer analysis, generating random point overlays is simple and is the primary method.

2.4.2 Photographic Equipment and Study Design

Surveys were conducted with Nikonos model V 35-mm cameras equipped with a 35-mm lens, an Ikelite Ai/n strobe light. Close-up (macro) images were obtained using extension rings and framing guides. Initially Ikelite 1:3 macro-rings and frames were used, but the system was very susceptible to leakage. Subsequently, Sea and Sea macro-ring and framing guide was employed with better results. The area photographed was 10.5 cm x 7.5 cm. This relatively small area was chosen for three main reasons: obtaining a high resolution image, minimizing turbid-water effects, and being roughly the same scale as scrape samples and artificial substrate plates.

The intended survey design was for four photographs to be taken at 5 depth intervals (1 m, 5 m, 10 m, 20 m, and 30 m) at 2 legs of each of the three study platforms. The four photographs would be taken at haphazard positions, two facing outward from the platform, and two facing the interior. Camera flooding, and general diving operation problems prevented the full design from being completed.

2.5 VIDEO SURVEY

Video surveying was incorporated into the study due to the effectiveness of the technique when employed by the TAMU-CC group submerged structure biotic surveys (Dokken et al. 2000). The appeal of the technique lies in the fact that the video record serves two purposes. The imagery provides information on platform biota that can be used to provide quantitative data and serves as a highly useful means of recording general aspects of the surveyed environment. As with photography, it frees the diver from tedious documentation and allows data production to be carried out once diving is finished. The primary limitation of the method arises from the medium to low resolution of video images.

2.5.1 Background of Video Survey Methods

Video surveying of the seafloor lagged behind photographic surveying until development of a practical recording technology. Commercial recorders were first developed by Ampex in 1956, but were far too expensive and fragile for use in field ecology. Cassette systems were not introduced until the 1970's. By the early 1980's, the video home system (VHS) developed and widely licensed by JVC had become predominant. Electronic miniaturization facilitated development of small consumer-grade cameras that could be easily housed for underwater use by SCUBA divers.

The introduction of Hi-8 camcorders in the late 1980's offered diving scientists a moderate-cost means of recording at very good horizontal resolution. Standard protocols for transect video survey have been adopted for reef studies by US workers (Rogers et al. 1994). The reef surveys of Aronson (Aronson et al. 1994) and Carlton and Done (1995) were instrumental in establishing these standards.

The utility of video camera's and recorders has, however, always suffered from problems of resolution. Video resolution is a confusing topic due to inconsistent use of "horizontal and vertical" and intentional misrepresentation in advertising. The National Television Standards Committee (NTSC) strictly limits vertical resolution, the number of lines counted vertically on a video monitor. That standard consists of 525 lines scanned in 1/30 of a second. However, only 480 scan lines are actually displayed. The undisplayed lines contain non-image information. An added degree of complexity arises from fact that the lines are not displayed in a simple progression (progressive scan). The over-the-air radio broadcast bandwidth adopted early in television's history, and the fading rate of early TV-tube phosphors resulted in a flickering image when progressive scan was used. To overcome this limitation, TV images are interlaced, meaning that odd lines are shown first followed by even lines. In order to be compatible

8

with US video monitors and TV's all videotape formats have the same NTSC vertical resolution (480 lines displayed out of 525) and the display is interleaved.

Horizontal resolution in video refers to the number of vertical lines that can be counted horizontally using the NTSC standard. Alternately, it can be thought of as the number of distinct dots that can be seen along each scan line. The number of these dots is much more variable than the NTSC mandated scan lines. The shadow mask or aperture grate in the display monitor sets the upper limit of horizontal resolution.

Interlacing of two fields to create a single frame imposes limits on the crispness of an image if there is any motion of the object or the camera. At a normal shutter speed of 1/60 of a second (exposure for a single field), NTSC video cameras take 2/60 of a second to record a single full frame. The part of the image displayed in adjacent scan lines is 1/60 of a second apart in time. Thus, if there is movement, even relatively slow movement, the displayed object will show shifts between the lines. This appears as a blurred margin to the viewer. This interlacing blur due to movement is much less noticeable when viewing video than in digitized still images since the eye and brain clean up motion blur very effectively. Methods of working around interlace blur to create images that are easier to analyze all have shortcomings. Most depend upon digitizing only one field (240 scan lines) of the NTSC scan then building the missing lines from the information in digitized lines. Depending on the nature of the image recorded, these algorithms can induce substantial blur and jaggedness.

At the time of writing of this report, consumer-grade video equipment is undergoing a transition from analog to digital. Most video cameras are now fully digital in the sense of producing a tape of digital image data. Unfortunately, playback and display are still restrained by the NTSC standards in order to be compatible with american television sets. The Moving Picture Coding Experts Group (MPEG) has defined the digital equivalent of the NTSC image as a 704 x 480 pixel array (MPEG-2). The 704 pixels along each scan line, however, are a much higher resolution than analog camera's are capable of producing. MPEG-2 is supported by most computer editing and playback software and equipment. High definition digital video is available with a dramatically improved resolution of 1440 x 1080 pixels, but equipment that can handle the required data transfer rates without unacceptable levels of image compression will not be available at reasonable costs until analog television has been more fully replaced by digital.

2.5.2   Video Equipment and Design

Surveys were to be conducted on the same two legs at each platform where photographs and other samples were taken. The equipment was a Sony TR-700 Hi8 Video camera housed in a Stingray underwater housing employing Sunray halogen lights for illumination. SCUBA divers would attempt to maintain a fairly constant 0.5 m distance from the leg, surveying vertically between depths of 1, 5, 10, 20, and 30 m except at ST-54 where 20 m would be the deepest. At these fixed depths, the diver would video around the circumference of the leg.

Video analysis consisted of playing the tapes on a Sony EVO-9700 video editor. Frames were captured for computer analysis using a Data Translation video capture board. Captured images were displayed on a DEC alpha workstation. The graphic capabilities of PV-WAVE software were used to superimpose 100 random points for classification. During the vertical surveying, an image was captured approximately every 1 second. During the horizontal survey, 5 adjacent images were captured. The area of the image varied from 0.5 to 0.25 m^2, estimated from the images of known objects. Lacking a fixed frame of reference, no area correction was applied.

2.6   SCRAPE SAMPLING

Scraping of biota from platform legs has been an integral part of Gulf of Mexico surveys either as a primary method or as a ground truth for image-based surveys. Unlike image sampling, it provides specimens for identification and has the potential to sample the entire fouling crust rather than just the visible surface.

2.6.1 Background of Scraping Survey Methods

Scraping biota from a platform with a metal tool is a simple process, but one that is very difficult to quantify and to assure consistency. Quantification was attempted by George and Thomas (1979) and Fotheringham (1981) by sampling a pre-bagged area. The former employed a strapped on grab-like device, and the latter, hammer and chisel. The consistency problem arises from considerable differences in substrate rugosity and strength.

2.6.2 Scraping Method and Design

This study employed heavy metal paint scrapers used by hand to chip and pry the biofouling mat from platform legs. An attempt was made to scrape a 20 cm x 20 cm area. All freed material was quickly transferred into 0.5 mm nytex mesh bag. The bags were then clipped to a guideline for surface retrieval. Bagged samples were bulk preserved in buffered formalin and shipped ashore for hand sorting of specimens down to 1 mm.

Identification of algae poses special problems associated with the delicate nature of most species and the necessity of preparing microscope slides for identification. In preparation for the identification task, snorkel surveys were conducted at all three platforms specifically for collection of algae. The collected material was prepared for slide preparation at sea. The literature was reviewed and an updated species checklist prepared (Appendix A). An expert, Dr. Frank Shaunagessy, carried out this preparation. Actual identification of algae from samples was carried out by general technicians and student workers. Identification was limited to genus in the final analysis.

2.7 SETTLING PLATES

The intent of settling plates was to develop methodology applicable to larger-scale and longer-term studies for determination of the composition of the larval pool recruiting to the platforms. Conceptually, it may be possible to assess recruitment from the analysis of scraped samples by estimating age of the collected biota. This would, however, require extensive investigation of age-growth relationships for a great variety of species. When settling plates are used, it is a simple matter to monitor settlement. The primary drawback of artificial substrates is that settlement may be different than on the encrusted surfaces of fouling communities. For the study at hand, the advantages of plates were seen as outweighing the disadvantages.

2.7.1 Background of Settling Plate Methods

American and European freshwater ecologist pioneered the use of algal settling plates in the 1960's to monitor water-quality in polluted waters. Since that time, various types and designs of plate deployment have become commonplace in lakes and streams. Settling plates are seeing increased usage for detection of introduced species, especially the zebra mussel (Marsden and Lansky 2000). Whatever the exact application, the great appeal of the methods is that they eliminate much of the uncontrolled variation in the natural environment and they make quantification simple.

Marine use of artificial substrates has been highly varied and undertaken for a wide range of purposes. Settling plates or experimental modification of platform surfaces have been employed in all Gulf studies since Gunter and Geyer 1955. Most marine ecologists dismiss the method as being too far from natural systems (i.e. Smith and Rule 2002). Settling plates are, however, seen by some as a convenient means of studying settlement processes and larval availability, especially for barnacles (i.e. Pineda 1994) without the complexity of natural systems. As in the freshwater environment, artificial substrates eliminate some of the uncontrolled complexity of the natural environment. They must, however, introduce new factors (effects of size, shape, flow, texture) that are poorly known (Butman et al. 1988).

The great appeal of settling plates in biofouling research lies in the fact that plates allow determination of active recruitment in a very simple manner. Therefore, the method can be easily applied in large-scale studies. The criticism that plates are artificial systems is less of a concern since platforms themselves are artificial. Criticism that plates have unknown scale, hydrodynamic, and substrate-settlement effects are all valid. However, these effects can be studied by controlled variation of parameters, or could be kept constant in a large study through standardization. In spite of considerable usage in a variety of habitats and a range of taxa, there appears to be no comprehensive review of artificial substrate use. Therefore, each new investigation is based upon unpublished prior experience, materials availability, and deployment logistics.

2.7.2 Settling Plate Method and Design

Plates consisted of a 17 cm by 17 cm square cut from quarter inch gray polyvinyl chloride sheet plastic. The size was selected for handling needs and production yield from 4' x 8' stock sheets of PVC. The surface of the plates were deglazed with deglazing solution to remove manufacturing residues and then roughed with a rotary sander. Mounting holes were drilled in two opposing corners. Six plates were spaced along a 2" wide nylon cargo ratchet strap so as to be evenly spaced when placed around a platform leg. Attachment of plates to the strap was by means of heavy-duty plastic cable ties fed through the plate holes and holes punched in the belt and reinforced with grommets. Two divers would carry the belt to the desired depth, circle the platform leg and tighten the belt in place with the ratchet mechanism. This arrangement allowed individual plates to be harvested and replaced.

Two modifications of an initial plan were made due to practical considerations. First, PVC plates were used rather than ceramic. The appeal of ceramic tile is that they could be custom manufactured with any desired surface texture and mounting holes preformed rather than drilled. During development of a deployment system, however, it was determined that breakage and weight during shipment and diver installation would be major problems. Comparably lightweight and unbreakable substrates could be made from plastics. Second, the ratchet belt system proved vulnerable to dislodgement by strong swell. Belts deployed at 1-m depth were routinely lost, but those deeper survived. Therefore, 1-m belts were replaced with one-inch chains.

Plates were harvested by diver and placed into a bag made of 250-micrometer nylon netting and ballistic nylon cloth. The bagged plates were put into 5-gallon pails on the surface. The pail was filled with 10% formalin solution and shipped by supply boat to the LSU campus. Within two weeks of arriving on campus, the formalin was poured off and replaced by 80% ethanol solution. In the lab, plates were washed over a 250-micrometer screen to catch mobile fauna, photographed to provide a long-term record of condition, and the biota enumerated by point counting. Bulk preserved scraping samples will be washed over a 250-micrometer screen to remove formaldehyde and hand sorted at 10X magnification. Invertebrates and algae will be separated to the lowest possible taxonomic level based on morphology. The design followed the overall sampling plan of three platforms, two legs, and depths of 1, 5, 10, 20 m at all platforms and 30 m at the deeper two.

3   SURVEY RESULTS

3.1   GENERAL SUCCESS OF FIELD EFFORTS

A dive team lead by James Tolan visited platforms six times (GC-18), five times (GI-94), and only two times (ST-54) between Nov. 1995 and Sept. 1997. All planned components were completed with some degree of success (Table 3-1). Dependence on diver teams working from three specific platforms, however, proved far more restrictive than anticipated. Bad weather limited the access to platforms, and once on platforms, weather limited diving. Conflicts with platform operations also severely limited access and dive operations. The most important impact was the loss of time series sampling. For the most part, video, and photography was used only once successfully at the platforms. No successful photographs of GC-18 were taken. Scraping was successful at all platforms, but without a time series. Plates were deployed at all platforms. Interval harvesting and deployment of new plates was carried out at GC-18 and GI-94. Unfortunately, no plates were harvested from ST-54 due to platform operations that would preclude safe diving for the duration of the project.

Table 3-1

Timing of Successful Operations at Platforms

Platform	Trip	Successful activity
Grand Isle 94	Nov. 95	Plates deployed
	Apr. 96	Plates redeployed
		Photography
	May 96	Plates redeployed
	Aug. 96	Plates redeployed
		Scrapes
		Video
	May 97	Plate harvest—final
Green Canyon 18	Jan. 96	Plates deployed
	Apr. 96	Plates redeployed
		Video
	May 96	Plates redeployed
	Sept. 96	Plates redeployed
		Scrapes
	Nov. 96	Plates redeployed
	Sept. 97	Plate harvest—final
South Timbalier 54	June 96	Plates deployed
		Scrapes
	July 96	Video
		Photography

3.2   VIDEO SURVEY

ST-54 and GI-94 were surveyed on two legs as planned. Thirty-seven and 48 images were captured from the two respectively. GC-18 was only partially surveyed on a single leg due to camera problems, diver time constraints, and unanticipated scheduling conflict with platform maintenance activities. Thirty eight images were captured from GC-18 from 5- to 30-m depths. When video was recorded in the vicinity of a fouling panel belt, depth was confidently known. Depths between belts were estimated from time. Platform structure complicated consistent videoing around the platform legs. Therefore, position (facing in or facing out) was not examined as a factor.

While the video did provide excellent illustration of the encrusting and fish fauna of the platform, quantification proved difficult, especially at ST-54 where visibility was limited. The poor resolution of the captured image combined with the substrate masking by bushy epifauna made identification very difficult. The categories used for image classification were

1. Bare—smooth surface of platform leg clearly visible.
2. Turf—a catchall term for an encrusted area for which no specific determination could be made.
3. Barnacles—included points falling in and close to the aperture of a barnacle. Overgrowths frequently masked the extent of barnacle cover.
4. Standing Sponges—sponges clearly extending from substrate.
5. Encrusting Sponges—mats identified by red to yellow color.
6. Bryozoans—white thin mats.
7. Hydroids—low to bush-like colonial polyps.
8. Anemones—larger encrusting individual polyps.
9. Bivalves—shell edges clearly visible.
10. Algae—thin translucent green to reddish-brown films.
11. Tunicates—colonies of ovoid bodies.
12. Bacterial Film—grey film observed only at ST-54.

Analysis of percent cover based upon point counting of digitized frames sought to determine if the three platforms showed vertical patterns within platform and inter-platforms biotic differences. Since vertical patterns might confound inter-platform patterns, it was examined first by means of simple Pearson product moment correlation coefficients (Tables 3-2, 3-3, and 3-4). Data are presented in Appendix B.

Table 3-2

Correlation Coefficients with Depth and Among Biofouling Categories at South Timbalier 54

ST-54	Depth	Bare	Turf	Barnacle	Bacterial Film	Sponge2	Hydroid	Bryozoa	Tunicate	Bivalve	Algae	Anemone
Depth	1.0000											
Bare	**-0.4203**	1.0000	-0.1289	0.1604	-0.2056	-0.2071	-0.1602				0.3091	
Turf	0.1580		1.0000	**-0.5879**	-0.2824	0.1126	-0.2971				-0.0533	
Barnacle	-0.0461			1.0000	**0.4336**	**-0.4811**	**-0.4759**				0.0250	
Bacterial	**0.7685**				1.0000	-0.3348	**-0.4708**				-0.3285	
Sponge 2	-0.0420					1.0000	0.2483				-0.1533	
Hydroid	-0.3257						1.0000				-0.0036	
Bryozoa												
Tunicate												
Bivalve												
Algae	**-0.5742**	0.3091	-0.0533	0.0250	-0.3285	-0.1533	-0.0036				1.0000	
Anemone												
n=37 Significant r > 0.3700 α = .90 Bold Faced												

14

Table 3-3

Correlation Coefficients with Depth and Among Biofouling Categories at Grand Isle 94

GI-94	Depth	Bare	Turf	Barnacle	Sponge1	Sponge2	Hydroid	Bryozoa	Tunicate	Bivalve	Algae	Anemone
Depth	1.0000											
Bare	**-0.3591**	1.0000	-0.3212	**0.4316**	**0.4569**	-0.1906	-0.1862	-0.1606	-0.0673	-0.0566		
Turf	-0.0245		1.0000	-0.2896	-0.2707	-0.2283	0.2210	-0.2532	-0.2098	0.1951		
Barnacle	**-0.4278**			1.0000	0.0614	-0.1574	-0.1592	-0.2377	-0.1089	-0.0919		
Sponge 1	**-0.3930**				1.0000	-0.1964	-0.2114	-0.1837	-0.0770	-0.0647		
Sponge 2	0.3041					1.0000	-0.2749	-0.2631	-0.1259	0.0674		
Hydroid	-0.0737						1.0000	-0.0733	-0.1982	-0.0958		
Bryozoa	0.1975							1.0000	-0.1385	-0.1196		
Tunicate	0.2596								1.0000	-0.0440		
Bivalve	0.3175									1.0000		
Algae												
Anemone												
n=48 Significant r >0.3300 α = 0.90 Bold Faced												

Table 3-4

Correlation Coefficients with Depth and Among Biofouling Categories at Green Canyon 18

GC-18	Depth	Bare	Turf	Barnacle	Sponge1	Sponge2	Hydroid	Bryozoa	Tunicate	Bivalve	Algae	Anemone
Depth	1.0000											
Bare	0.0763	1.0000	-0.1245	0.2783		-0.1563	-0.0984	0.1631		**0.4408**	0.3108	-0.1098
Turf	-0.1171		1.0000	-0.0727		-0.3556	0.0350	-0.0319		0.0211	0.1540	-0.1229
Barnacle	0.2552			1.0000		-0.0740	0.1264	0.1064		0.1967	-0.1351	-0.2456
Sponge 1												
Sponge 2	0.2976					1.0000	-0.2157	-0.0585		-0.1392	-0.2609	-0.1131
Hydroids	**0.5793**						1.0000	**0.3741**		-0.1380	**-0.4875**	**-0.4138**
Bryozoa	**0.5445**							1.0000		-0.0507	-0.3312	-0.2096
Tunicate												
Bivalve	-0.0059									1.0000	0.3058	-0.1346
Algae	**-0.6152**										1.0000	**0.4824**
Anemone	**-0.5955**											1.0000
n=38 Significant r > 0.3700 α = 0.90 Bold Faced												

At ST-54 vertical zonation is evident from the significant correlations between depth and bare areas, bacterial film, and algae. The negative correlation with algae is consistent with decreasing light levels. The positive correlation with bacterial film is consistent with near-bottom hypoxia. The negative correlation with bare patches may reflect more frequent loss of barnacle patches due to greater wave surge near the surface. Significant correlations among biotic categories are all negative and may simply reflect overgrowth such that turf, sponges, and hydroids obscure barnacles. Near bottom on the platform bacterial films obscure the small hydroids but not the larger barnacles.

At GI-94 vertical zonation is evidenced by the significant negative correlations between depth and bare patches, barnacles, and stalked sponges (Table 3-3). All three decrease with depth. The only significant correlations among categories are between bare patches, barnacles ands stalked sponges. This may simply reflect the common response to depth. Unexpectedly, stalked sponges and barnacles show no significant correlation. This is mostly likely due to patchy distribution and the fact that the stalked sponges do not obscure the underlying barnacles.

Simple vertical zonation of biota at GC-18 is evidenced from correlation analysis (Table 3-4). Hydroids and bryozoans are highly variable but increase significantly with depth. Algae and anemones show the opposite trend, decreasing in percent cover. Of the significant correlations among cover types, hydroid-bryozoa and algae-anemone simply reflect the common effects of depth. The positive correlation between bivalves and bare areas is the only other significant correlation. There are two likely causes, both dealing with unmasking of the mollusks. First, areas that appear bare may be due to recent stripping of outer encrusting animals, exposing the large cemented bivalves. Second, apparently bare areas may actually be created by bivalves falling from the substrate in areas of high bivalve populations.

Vertical zonation was evident from videos at all three platforms. The patterns were primarily platform specific with only two suggestions of general patterns. Algae decreased with depth except where not confidently identified at GI-94. This is consistent with reduced light at depth, but may also represent grazing pressure differences. Bare patches decreased with depth except at GC-18. If the presence of patches in the shallower platforms reflect greater wave-associated current velocities, the most offshore platform may reflect lower velocities associated with greater bottom depths.

Statistical assessment of inter-platform similarity is made somewhat problematic due to the presence of significant but inconsistent vertical differences. An ANOVA partitioned by depth and platform would have significant interaction terms and be made unbalanced due to the narrower depth range at the shallow ST-54 platform. Therefore, analyses were limited to simpler examination of similarity among platforms (Figure 3.1). The video data somewhat resemble the zonation narrative of Gallaway and Lewbel (1982). Barnacles are most important nearshore at ST-54. Bivalves increased offshore, but were not as visually important as sponges. Results at all three platforms showed a limitation of medium-resolution video, the large unresolved "turf" comprised from 24% to 33% of the area classified.

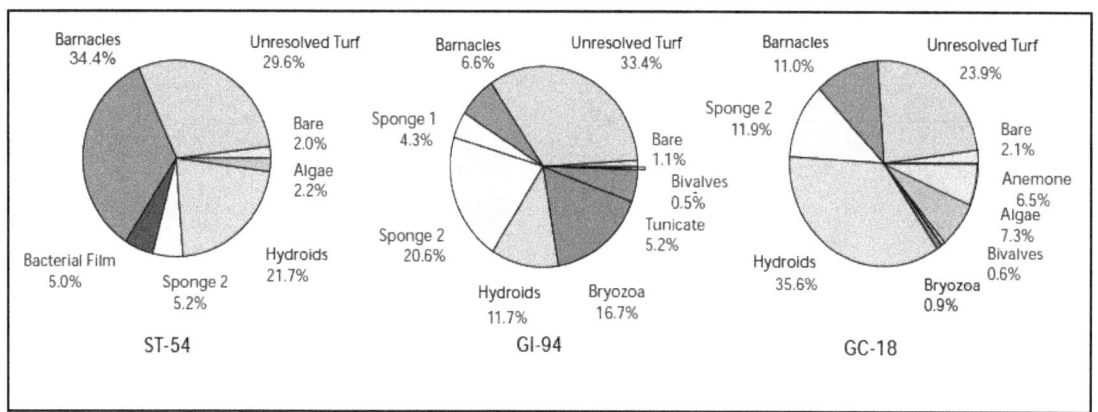

Figure 3.1. Pie charts of average percent cover determined from digitized Hi-8 video surveys of platform legs.

3.3   35-MM PHOTOGRAPHIC SURVEYS

Successful photographic surveys were completed on two legs of ST-54 on a single visit and two legs of GI-94 during two visits. Water and light leaks ruined other attempts. No surveys were conducted at GC-18 due to early equipment problems and later dive time restrictions. A total of 102 useful images were obtained. Visually, the two platforms were extremely different. ST-54 was covered by a dense barnacle crust overlain with a dark covering only a few millimeters thick. The covering did not obscure the underlying barnacles, although it did make species identification unreliable. Diversity at this inshore structure appeared to be low. GI-94 images most often were dominated by extensive overgrowths of sponge, hydroids, and corals completely obscuring the underlying organisms/structures. Diversity appeared to be higher at this mid-shelf structure.

Due to the large number of images and categories (30) of biota observed, cluster analysis was used as a simple means of assessing intra- and inter-platform patterns. Similarity was calculated as simple

Euclidean distance on untransformed counts. Clustering of the similarity matrix was carried out using the flexible clustering algorithm.

Given the dramatic visual differences between the darkly overgrown barnacles and ST-54 and the bright sponge and hydroid-covered surfaces at GI-94, it was no surprise that cluster analysis of all images produced two major clusters (Figure 3.2). All but three ST-54 images clustered together as a relatively homogenous group. The three exceptions all occurred at 5 m depth and had large areas obscured by shadows due to rugosity. Most GI-94 images clustered in a single less homogenous cluster with several isolated small clusters reflecting the greater visual diversity at that platform. Depth, position in versus out and cruise had no noticeable patterns. Unequal sampling, however, weakened the ability to detect all within-platform patterns other than depth.

Patterns within platforms such as depth, position at a fixed depth, and time (two series at GI-94) were also examined by the same cluster analysis. At GI-94, two main clusters were created mainly on the basis of the percent of sponge cover and unidentifiable area (Figure 3.3). Depth, times, and positions were mixed without obvious pattern. ST-54 showed a similar split into two clusters based mostly on the percentage of barnacle cover (Figure 3.4). Again depth and position did not have obvious patterns. The overall impression of photographic images is that biota is patchy rather than cleanly divided into depth zones.

An unanticipated problem with close-up images was the extreme complexity of overgrowths. Most often, all large fauna found in scrape samples were completely obscured by covering films. Unfortunately, the exact identification of the films could not be determined from scrapes. Typically, the films were easily destroyed during scraping, and seemed to consist of relatively few layers of algal cells, other microbes, and hydroid fecal material. For the purpose of analysis, films were classed by color.

3.4 SCRAPE SAMPLES

Scraping produced 86 samples from all three platforms. One meter depth samples proved hard to get due to wave surge. Thirty meter samples proved hard to obtain due to dive time considerations and the shallow depth of ST-54. Rather than treat all the scarped biota simultaneously, it was considered more informative to partition the data into three functional groups (Appendix B).

1. Substrate-Forming—these are the carbonate depositing barnacles and bivalves that form the major component of the encrusting mat.

2. Overgrowths—these are colonial forms such as bryozoa, sponge, algae, hydroids, etc. generally found as the outermost layer atop substrate-forming species.

3. Free-living—these are mobile organisms living within and upon the mat including amphipods, decapods, isopods, ophiuroids, etc.

Due to the large size and strength of the shelled organisms, they are relatively well sampled by scraping. When firmly attached to this shelled substrate, overgrowth organisms are also well sampled. Some, however, formed semi-attached, neutrally buoyant layers that were broken and scattered into the water column during rough scraping. Sampling of free-living forms has to be considered fortuitous with only specimens trapped in the structure of the mat making it into a sample bag. Due to the distinctiveness of the categories and unevenness of sampling, each group was analyzed separately.

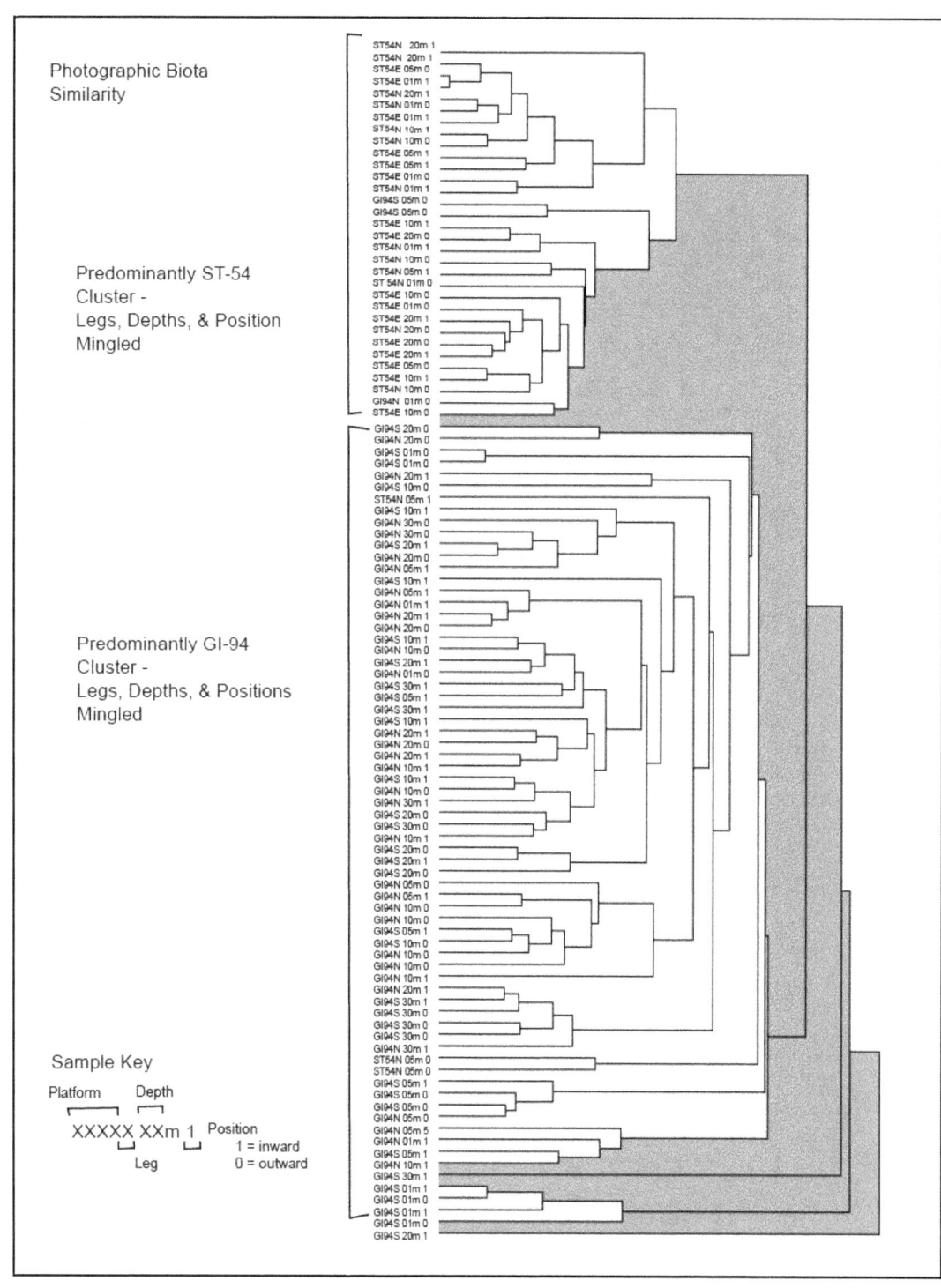

Figure 3.2. Cluster analysis of all photographs at ST-54 and GI-94 platforms.

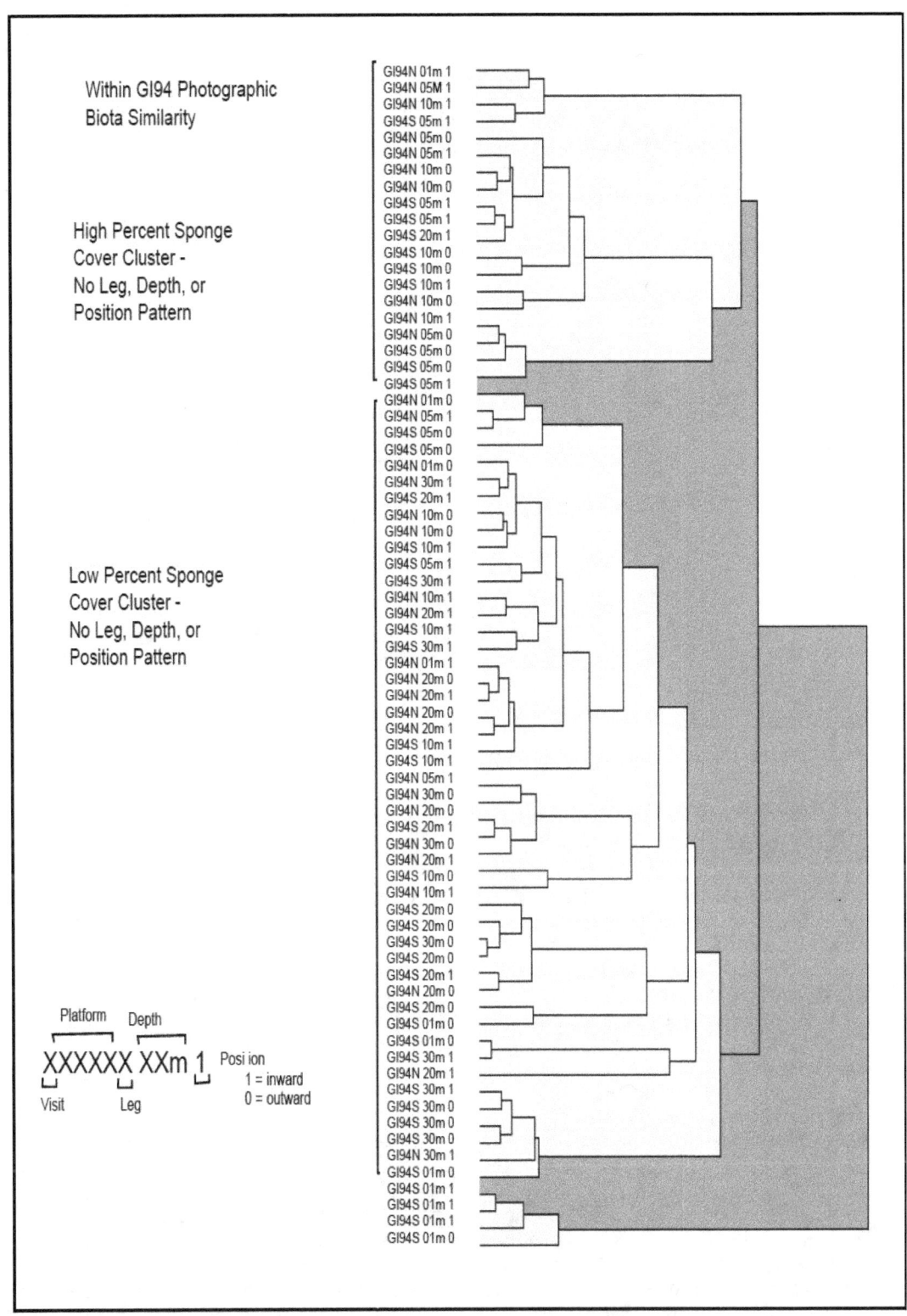

Figure 3.3. Cluster analysis GI-94 photos only

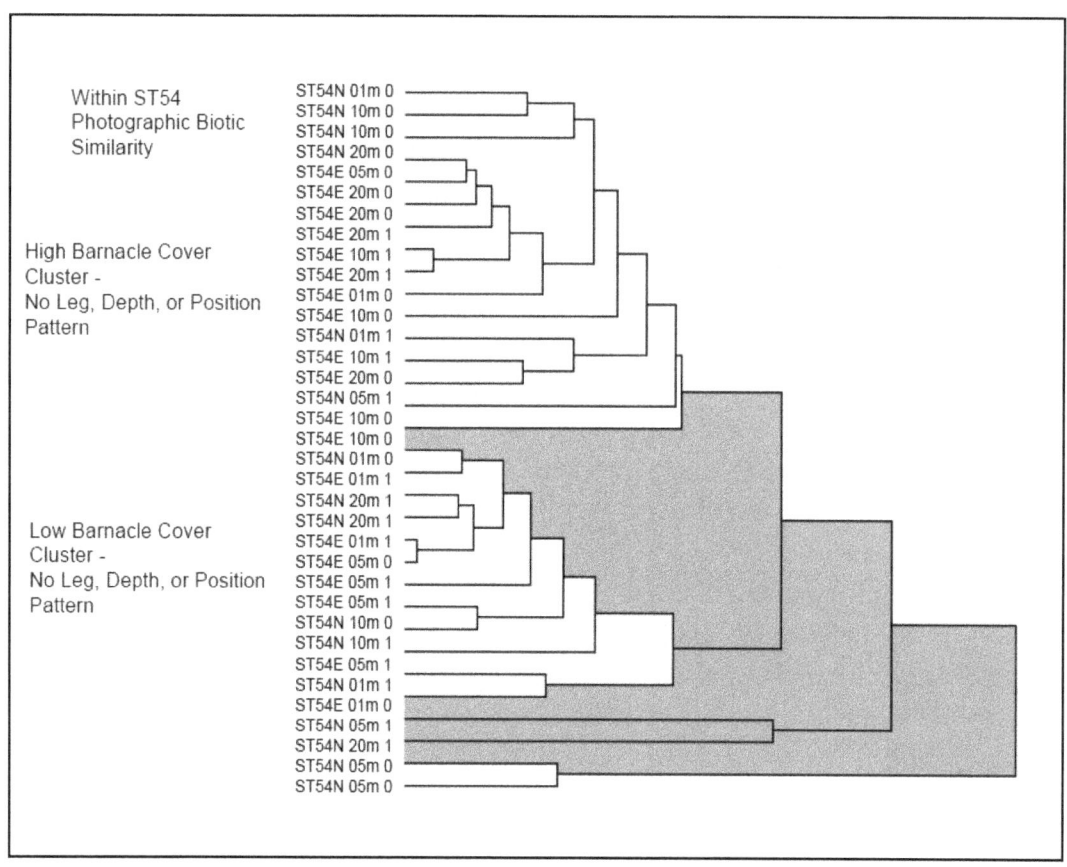

Figure 3.4. Cluster analysis of ST-54 photos only

3.4.1 Substrate-Forming Fauna Results

The epifaunal crust on all three platforms consisted on a site-specific mix of balanoid barnacles, cementing bivalves, and byssate bivalves. Gittings et al. (1986) was used as the primary source for identification of the barnacles. Cementing and byssate bivalves were identified to genus using the keys of Coan et al. (2000) and to species using the descriptions in Abbott (1953). Due to the large number of small barnacle specimens, only the identity of dominant species were determined at each site and then all barnacles enumerated without identification. ST-54 was dominated by *Balanus reticulatus*. *B. eburneus* and *B. improvisus* were present in lower numbers. The larger *Megabalanus antillensis* formed scattered clusters. GI-94 had conspicuous large clumps of *M. antillensis* with much smaller *Balanus trigonus* attached. GC-18 had similar clumps of *M. antillensis*. *B. trigonus*, and an unidentified balanoid that may be young *M. antillensis*.

There is still some taxonomic instability in the barnacles. Gallaway and Lewbel (1982) expressed the opinion that *B. reticulatus* should be correctly identified as *B. amphitrite* and is the coastal dominant off Louisiana. That work identified the conspicuous large barnacles as *Megabalanus (Balanus) tintinabulum*. Gittings et al. (1986), however, implicitly reject the *reticulatus-amphitrite* confusion, and list *B. reticulatus* as the dominant form. The utility of morphological identification of barnacles in the Gulf of Mexico may have reached its limit, and molecular identification may now be the required tool.

The cementing bivalves were easily identified on the basis of shell morphology and abductor muscle number. ST-54 scrape samples yielded only small specimens, possibly in the genus *Crassostrea*. GI-94 and GC-18 both had numerous specimens of *Chama macerophylla* and *Lopha frons*. Divers observed and collected incidental specimens of *Spondylus americanus* at GC-18, but none were found in the scrape and settlement samples of the formal design. The thick basal valves of these animals were usually occupied by burrowing mussels of the genus *Lipthophaga*. Two species were present, *L. aristata* and *L.* cf.

20

a*ntillarum*, but shell damage during collecting and freeing from the carbonate matrix made identification past the genus impossible for most specimens.

The bivalves attached by byssal fibers were easily identified by overall morphology. ST-54 had only a few specimens of *Isognomen bicolor*. This animal was far more common at GI-94 and GC-18 forming dense clumps attached to cementing bivalves. Arcidae were also present. *Barbatia candida* was very rare at ST-54, but more common at GI-94 and GC-18. Large specimens of *Arca zebra* were found only at GI-94. Byssal holdfasts were common on cementing bivalves indicating that many arcids may have fallen from samples during collecting. A single specimen of *Pinctata radiata*, the Atlantic pearl oyster was found at GI-94.

The carbonate crust-forming fauna found in this study differs somewhat from the zonation scheme proposed by Gallaway and Lewbel (1982). The increased importance of bivalves offshore was confirmed. However, the concomitant decrease in barnacle importance is not as great. Even at the GC-18 site, which should fall in the bluewater category, barnacles are still an important component of the platform ecosystem.

3.4.2   General Patterns of Carbonate-Depositing Fauna within Platforms

The distinctiveness of the substrate forming biota at the three platforms is readily apparent from cluster analysis (Figure 3.5). Data were normalized prior to analysis to reduce the influence of the dominant barnacles on the clustering. Samples taken in close proximity (same depth, same leg, and same side of leg) tend to cluster together, but not exclusively so. All except eight samples, each from GI-94 and GC-18, clustered into three larger groups. The largest cluster contains subgroups consisting primarily of ST-54 samples. The smallest cluster consisted primarily of GI-94 samples. The intermediate was a combination of samples from GI-94 and GC-18. Examination of the data showed that the separation of the inshore ST-54 samples was due to the preponderance of barnacles at that site and the exclusion of cemented bivalves such as *Chama* and the byssate *Arca*. The byssate bivalve I*sognomon bicolor* is abundant on the more offshore platforms, but does occur in patches at ST-54; thus the similarity between ST-54 and some GI-18 samples. The dissimilarity among some GC-18 and GI-94 samples is largely associated with the two species of Arcidae more prevalent at GI-94.

3.4.3   Intra-Platform Patterns of Carbonate Cementing Fauna

Depth and position patterns at each platform was examined by the same cluster analysis procedure. At ST-54, three distinct clusters were found based upon minor contributions to a relatively monotonous barnacle cover (Figure 3.6). Ten samples, which had tree oysters in addition to barnacles, formed on cluster with no consistent depth, leg, or position pattern. Two samples that contained boring mussels in a dense barnacle base clustered together, and the remaining 20 samples clustered together containing only barnacles. Samples in close proximity were often most similar, but the *Isognomon*-defined patches seemed scattered about the platform structure without definite zonation. It is the presence of tree oyster patches that resulted in some similarity with GC-18 samples.

At GI-94 two large clusters were found representing distinct combinations of bivalves and barnacles (Figure 3.7). Samples in which one or both species of *Arca* were relatively abundant formed a cluster of 13 samples. The other cluster was distinguished largely by the absence or rarity of these same species. Samples in close proximity were often most similar, but patches seemed scattered about the platform structure without definite zonation.

At GC-18 three main patches with one outlier were recognized (Figure 3.8). A large cluster of 15 samples shared the common trait of containing *Arca* sp. causing the similarity with GI-94. *A. zebra* was, however, missing, causing a dissimilarity. Further subdivision was based largely on the presence or absence of the boring mussel *Lithophaga* sp.

21

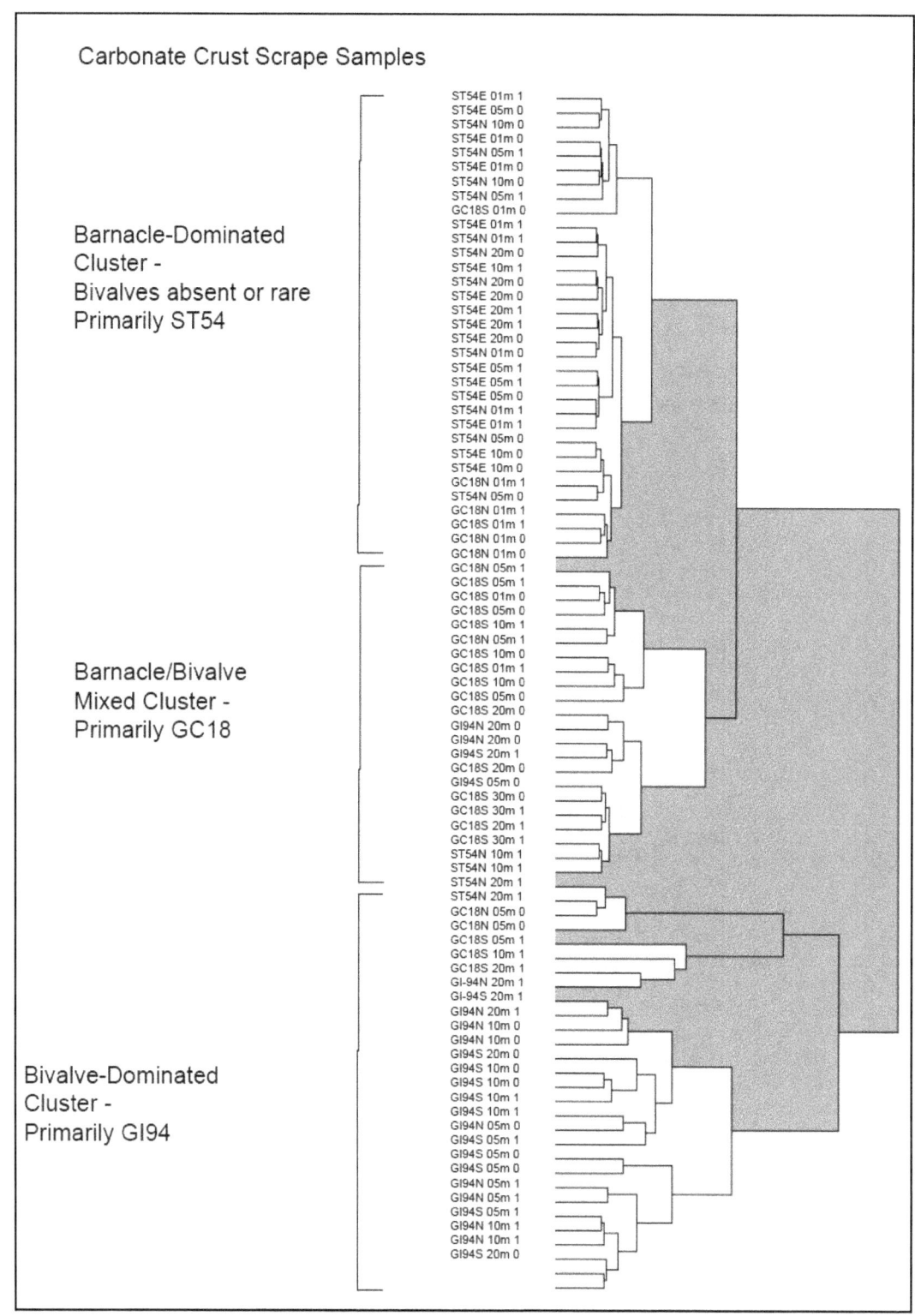

Figure 3.5. Cluster analysis of carbonate-forming fauna in scrape samples.

22

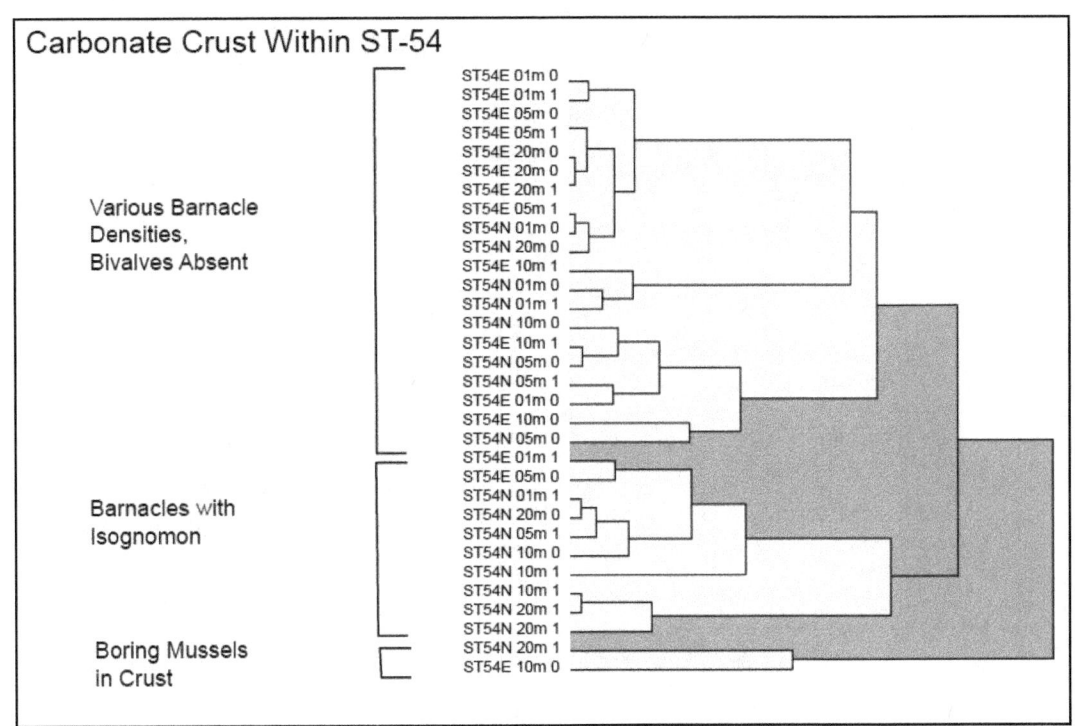

Figure 3.6. Results of cluster analysis ST-54 alone substrate-forming samples.

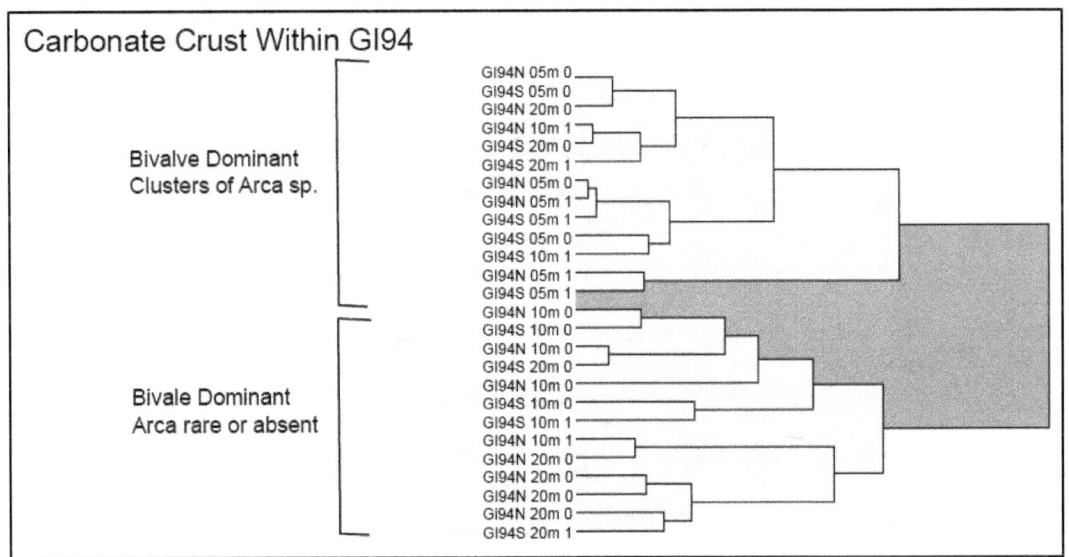

Figure 3.7. Results of cluster analysis GI-94 substrate-forming samples.

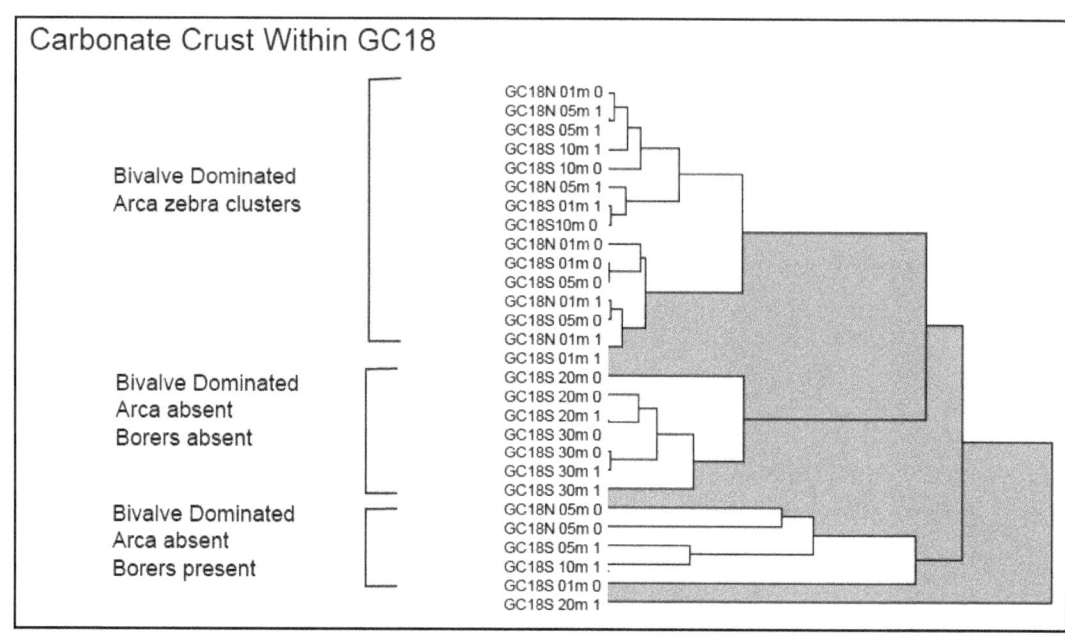

Figure 3.8. Results of cluster analysis GC-18 substrate-forming samples.

The abundance relationship among substrate-forming fauna was examined through calculation of product-moment correlation coefficients (Table 3-5). The few large correlations suggested that the fauna was not divided into distinct separate assemblages. Significant positive correlations were associated with the cementing bivalves *Chama pellucida* and *Lopha frons*. The high correlation between these and *Lithophaga* sp reflects the need of a substantial carbonate base for the boring mussel to survive. The consistently negative, but low correlation, of all species with barnacles is due to near absence of the other species at the inshore ST-54 site.

Table 3-5

Correlation among substrate-forming taxa

N=84	Barnacle	*Chama*	*Arca zebra*	*Barbatia*	*Lithophaga*	*Isognomon*	*Lopha*
Barnacle	1						
Chama	-0.3367	1					
Arca zebra	-0.1299	0.3962	1				
Barbatia sp	-0.2080	0.5501	0.4433	1			
Lithophaga	-0.2359	0.6348	0.4909	0.4163	1		
Isognomon	-0.2844	0.3597	-0.0609	0.3329	0.2385	1	
Lopha	-0.3070	0.6931	0.2096	0.4916	0.4562	0.3516	1

3.4.4 Mobile Fauna Results

Twenty-four mono-specific or poly-specific categories of mobile fauna were recognized. Amphipods were the most numerous and also diverse with eight distinct morpho-species. These were assigned numerical codes until specialized research can resolve taxonomic uncertainties. Juvenile and small decapod crabs were similarly diverse with eight species found and identified with confidence to species or genus. Six species of ophiuroids were found. Pycnogonids and isopods were represented by single species. Polychaetes tended to be small and badly fragmented; all were lumped into a single category and rough estimates made as to the number of specimens present.

The existence of consistent mobile fauna assemblages was examined through calculation of among-group correlation coefficients followed by cluster analysis. Distinct associations were not found (Figure 3.9). Due to the size of the 24 x 24 correlation matrix, the results are presented as a dendrogram. Especially noteworthy is the paucity of significant correlations; abundance among species was not closely related. The largest grouping of six taxa was found across all platforms but tended to be most abundant at ST-54. A cluster of five taxa were mostly associated with GC-18. Other taxa were scattered among the platforms without much pattern.

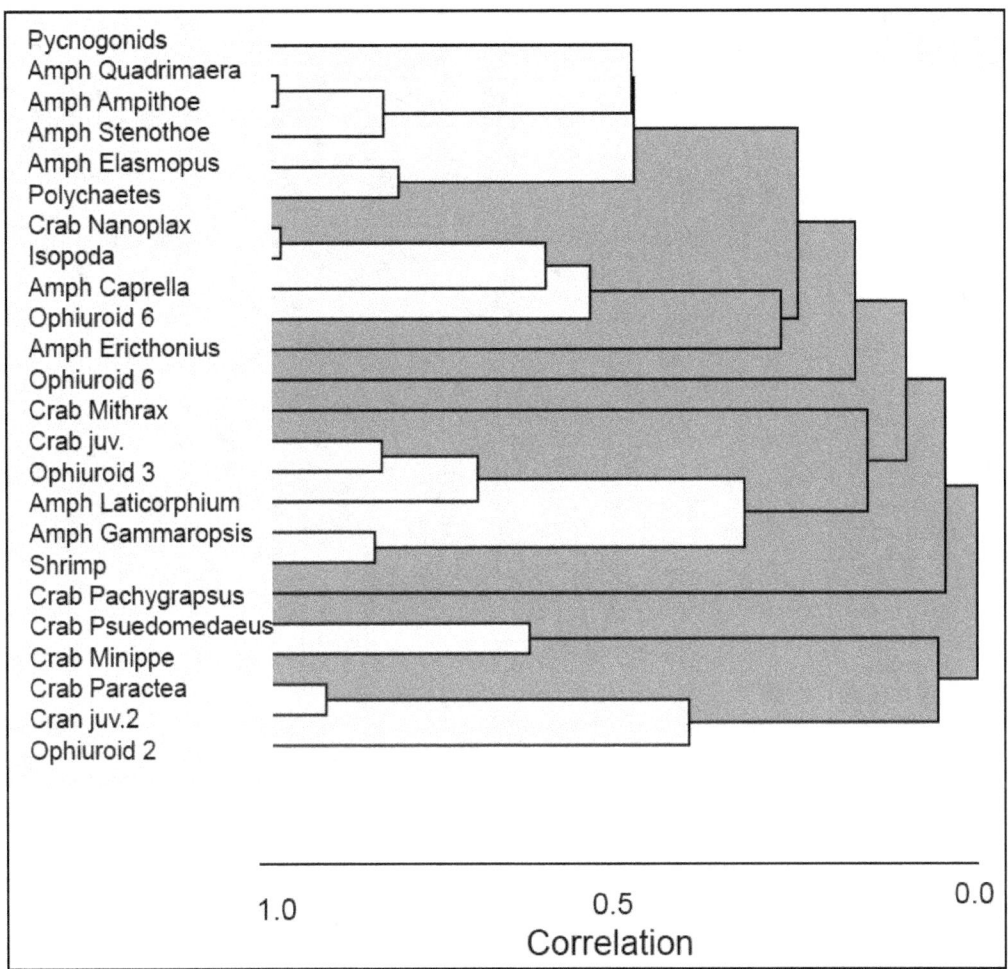

Figure 3.9. Correlations among mobile fauna presented as a cluster tree.

Inter-platform patterns in mobile fauna was examined by cluster analysis following data normalization. Two rather than three clusters were found (Figure 3.10). Both clusters are highly mixed, with samples from all platforms and most depths. One was predominantly the inshore ST-54 and the most offshore GC-18. The larger contained scrape samples from all platforms. There is very little obvious order in the distribution of mobile fauna taken as a whole.

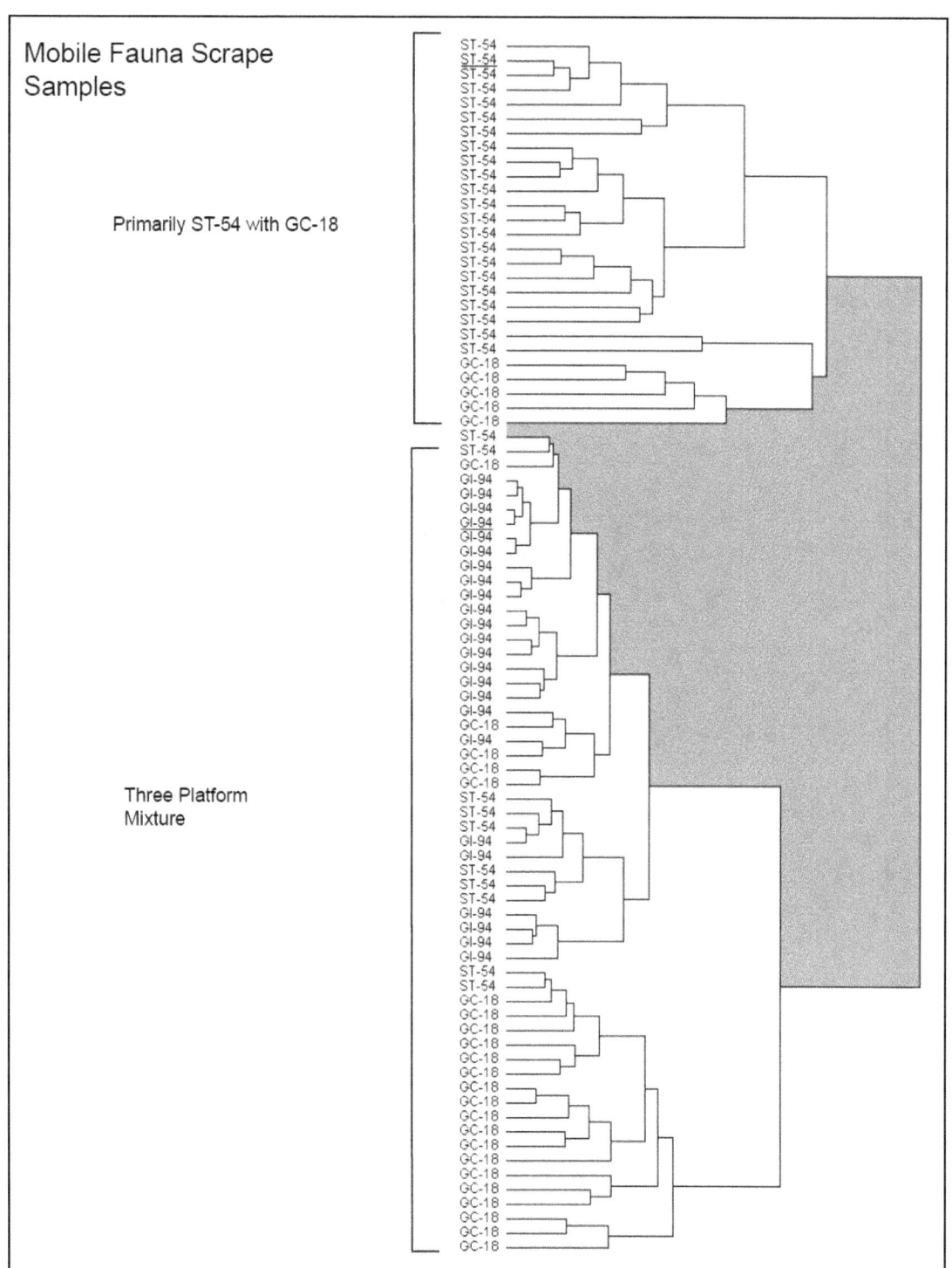

Figure 3.10. Cluster analysis of mobile fauna.

3.4.5 Results for Biotic Overgrowth

The surfaces of cementing species were almost universally covered with encrusting fauna when viewed in video and photographs. During scraping, however, much of this overgrowth was dislodged and broken in such a manner that in preserved samples it was reduced to a mixed debris. This posed a major problem for quantification. Information about area covered was lost upon collecting, and weight was split between a fraction still attached to hard substrate and a fraction completely mixed with miscellaneous debris. As a result, it was decided to record encrusting fauna only as presences and absence. Unfortunately, relative abundance information is lost, but artifacts of sampling and sample processing are largely eliminated.

Taxonomic support for identification of encrusting organisms is not well developed, depending upon the taxa under consideration. Most algae, especially filamentous film-forming species, required preparation of slides and high magnification. Shaunagessy's (Appendix A) updating of the Bert and Humm (1979) checklist combined with Schneider and Searle (1991) and Littler and Littler (2000) served to identify algae to genus in most cases. Identification of sponges to genus was attempted using Hooper and Wiedenmayer (1994) and a web-available companion guided (Hooper 2000). A more comprehensive volume (Hooper and Van Soest 2003) became available after completion of the identification phase. Ectoprocta (bryozoans) were identified with Canu and Bassler (1928); a newer revision and treatment is needed.

Thirty-two genera of algae (Appendix A) were identified from scrape samples. These were most abundant on 1- and 5-m samples and apparently absent at greater depths. Identification of sponges proved very difficult, and most material was simply classified as unidentified. The most common sponge encountered at GC-18 and GI-94 was a red to pink encrusting form commonly identified as *Diplestrella*; this identification could not be confirmed. The boring sponge *Cliona* also formed red mats. Brown mats of *Stelleta* were common at the ST-54 site. Patches of the blue *Halisarca* were occasionally encountered at the two offshore platforms. Hydrozoans were abundant with *Obelia* and *Turritopsis* being predominant forms in the thin mat found at ST-54. GI-94 and GC-18 lacked a similar mat, but had numerous colonies of *Bougainvilla*, *Eudendrium*, *Tubularia*, and *Sertularia*. A large number of specimens, especially the athecate forms, could not be identified from the bulk-preserved samples. Careful collection with relaxation prior to identification will be required. Hard corals were missing from the samples, but a soft coral identified as *Telesto* in Gallaway and Lewbell (1982) was common in small colonies. The most conspicuous ectoprocts (bryozoans) were low encrusting forms like *Membranipora*, *Aeverillia*, and *Parasmittina*. Stalked forms were limited to *Bugula*. Anemone patches were limited to the genus *Anthoplura*.

Since data on encrusting forms was limited to presence/absence, inter sample similarities were calculated with the Jaccard coefficient and clustering carried out via the flexible cluster algorithm. The results (Figure 3.11) are similar to those obtained from carbonate crust organisms with one important exception. As with carbonate forms, ST-54 has a distinct assemblage while GI-94 and GC-18 lump together. The difference is that shallower samples (1-5 m) at all sites are distinct from deeper. Thus there is distinct vertical zonation determined primarily by the light-limited algae.

3.5 PLATES

The settlement plate study was severely impacted by dive time restrictions and unanticipated platform activity. Deployments and recoveries at GI-94 went reasonably well. Renewed drilling and platform reconfiguration at GC-18 limited access and caused repeated loss of deployments; only partial recovery was possible. Renewed drilling at ST-54 prevented completion of the project, and none of the deployments were recovered. The resulting data allow informative analysis at GI-94 but do not support the desired inter-platform comparisons.

At GI-94 settlement plate installation was initiated on a NW corner leg on 15 Nov. 1995 with 24 plates successfully installed in belts of six at the design depths of 1, 5, 10, 20, and 30 m. Restrictions delayed installation on a similar set on a SE leg until 13 Feb. 1995. Plates were harvested and replaced on both legs during visits beginning 23 Apr. and 5 Aug. 1996. All plates were removed 21 May 1997. A total of 99 pates were harvested. Multiple constraints on diving impacted the deployment, harvest, and replacement schedule resulting in unbalanced data with respect to number of samples per leg, at each depth, and for each duration (Figure 3.12).

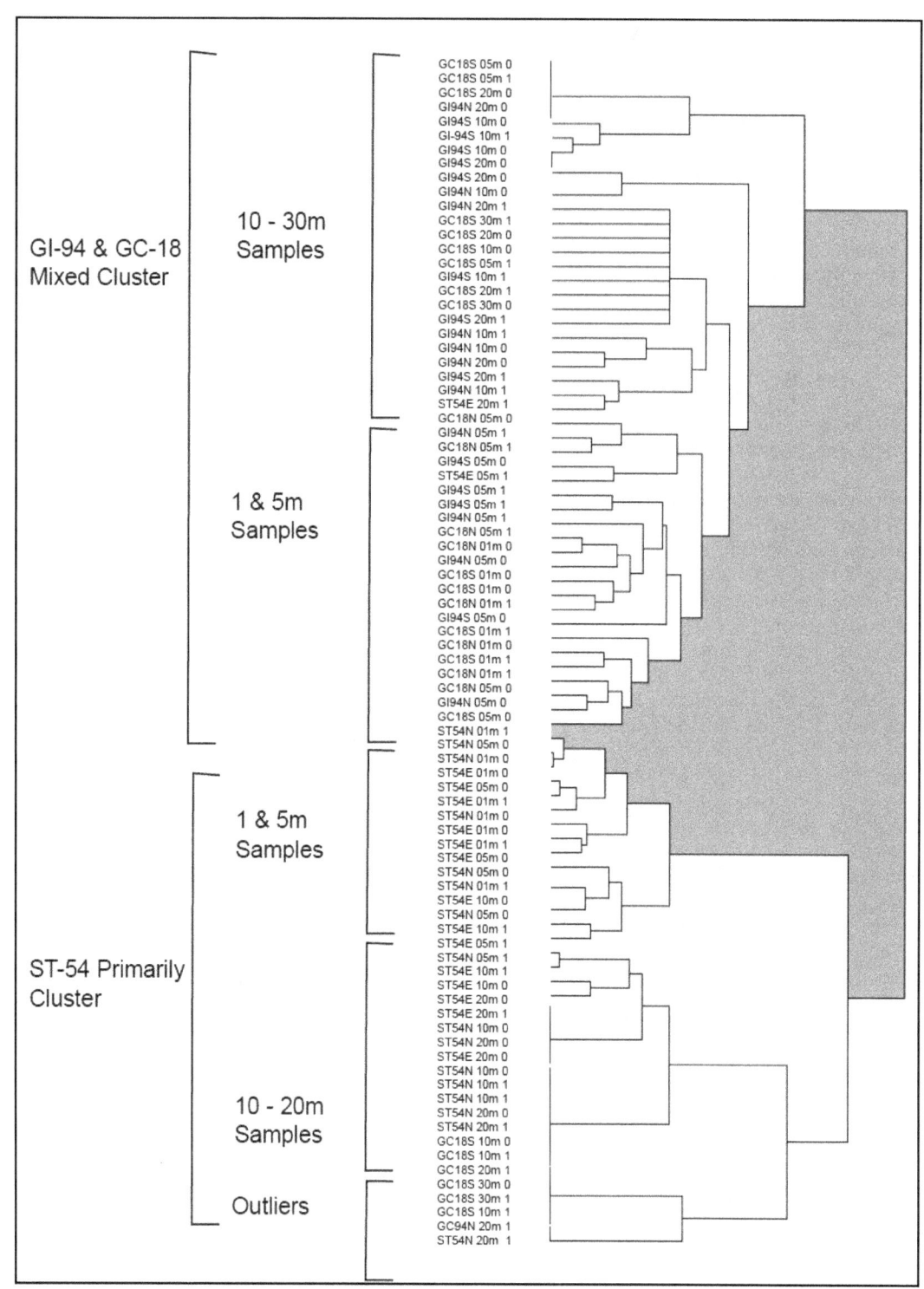

Figure 3.11. Cluster analysis for algal and invertebrate overgrowths.

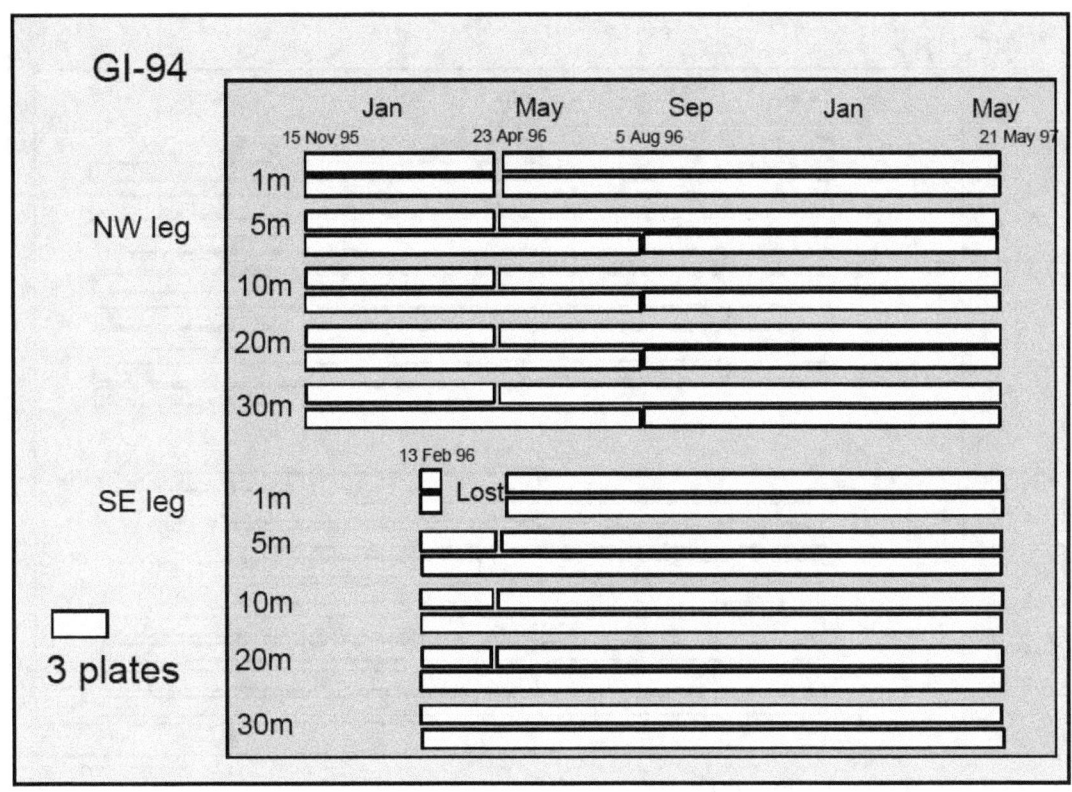

Figure 3.12. Schematic of settling plate deployment and harvest at GI-94. Each bar represents the history of a group of 3 plates.

At GC-18 installation was initiated Jan. 1996 on a NW and SE corner leg using belts of six plates at 1, 5, 10, 20, and 30 m. Both 1 m deployments were missing on 10 April 1996. Replacement with chains was delayed until Sept. Harvest, replacement, and repair activity took place during visits on 10 Apr. 1996, 9 September. 1996, and 18 Nov. 1996. Final harvest was carried out 17 Sept. 1997. During this interval, three individual plates were lost at 1m, and entire belts lost at 5 and 10m. The 1m losses may have been associated with wave surge. The deeper losses appear to have been associated with platform reconfiguration activity. A total of 66 plates were harvested with only one being lost during diving operations (Figure 3.13).

Plate deployments at ST-54 could not be initiated until June 96. Water depth limited deployments to 1, 5, 10, and 20 m. Harvesting was scheduled for May 97, but renewed drilling effectively terminated work at that platform. The plates were never recovered.

All plates were preserved in 10% formalin. Prior to analysis, plates were soaked in water for 48 hours. Plates were photographed for archival purposes. Attached fauna was identified while wet. Plates were air dried in a 30° C. drying oven and dry weight determined. Plates at GI-94 were predominantly covered with *Megabalanus antillensis* up to 1.5 cm in diameter and *Balanus trigonus* 3 mm and smaller. The most heavily fouled plate had two layers of large barnacles covering it. A bryozoa, *Membranipora* sp. was also common, covering up to 75% of bare plates and over growing barnacles. Plates at GC-18 had similar fauna, but were far more sparsely colonized. Sponge layers were more common, and 4 plates had single specimens of the tree oyster *Isognomon bicolor* attached.

29

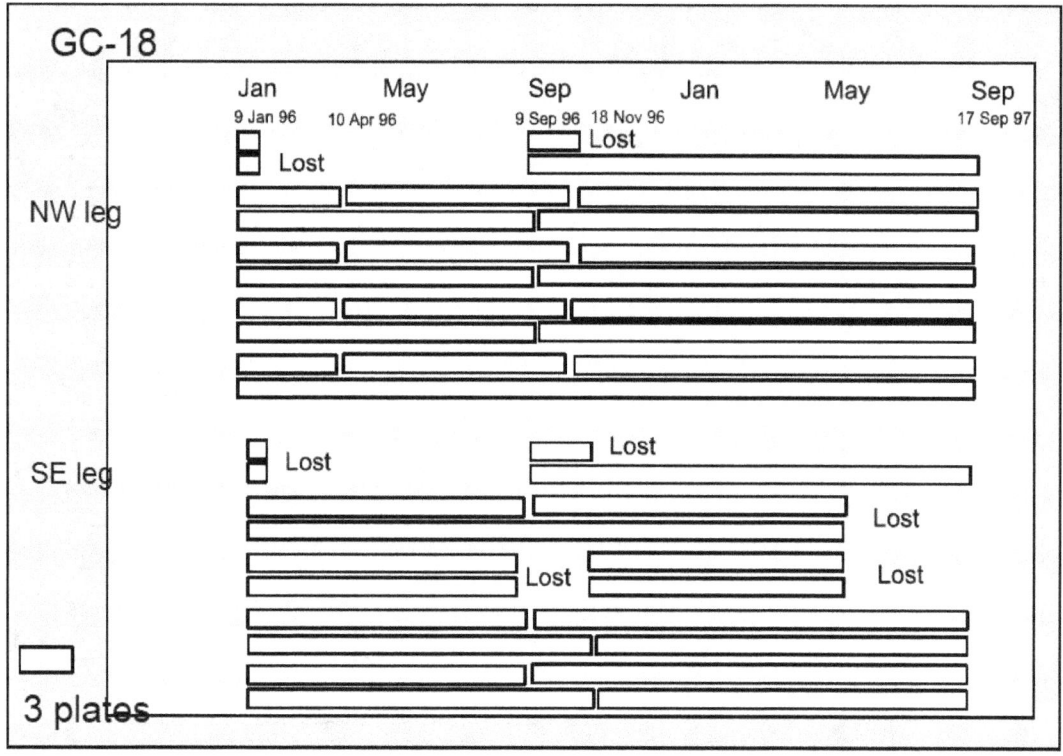

Figure 3.13. Schematic of settling plate deployment and recovery at GC-18.

The most informative data obtained from the settling plates were the extent of overall colonization measured as dry weight (Figure 3.14). At GC-18 and GI-94 the plates at each depth from both legs were combined for statistical examination. At GI-94 there was an obvious decline in dry weight with depth. A significant negative correlation with depth was found (r = -0.63) indicating that depth explains only 40% of the total variance in dry weight. At GC-18 a very similar pattern and negative correlation was also found (r = -0.45), but much less variance was associated with depth (~ 20%). Of particular interest are the higher dry weight values at GI-94 indicated by the intercept term in regression and the slower decrease with depth.

3.6 SPECIMEN ARCHIVING

An archive of preserved specimens has been established at Louisiana State University and is maintained by Dr. Carney. Identified exemplars are being submitted to the U.S. National Museum of Natural History through the department of Invertebrate Zoology. The taxa maintained are listed in the data tables of Appendix A.

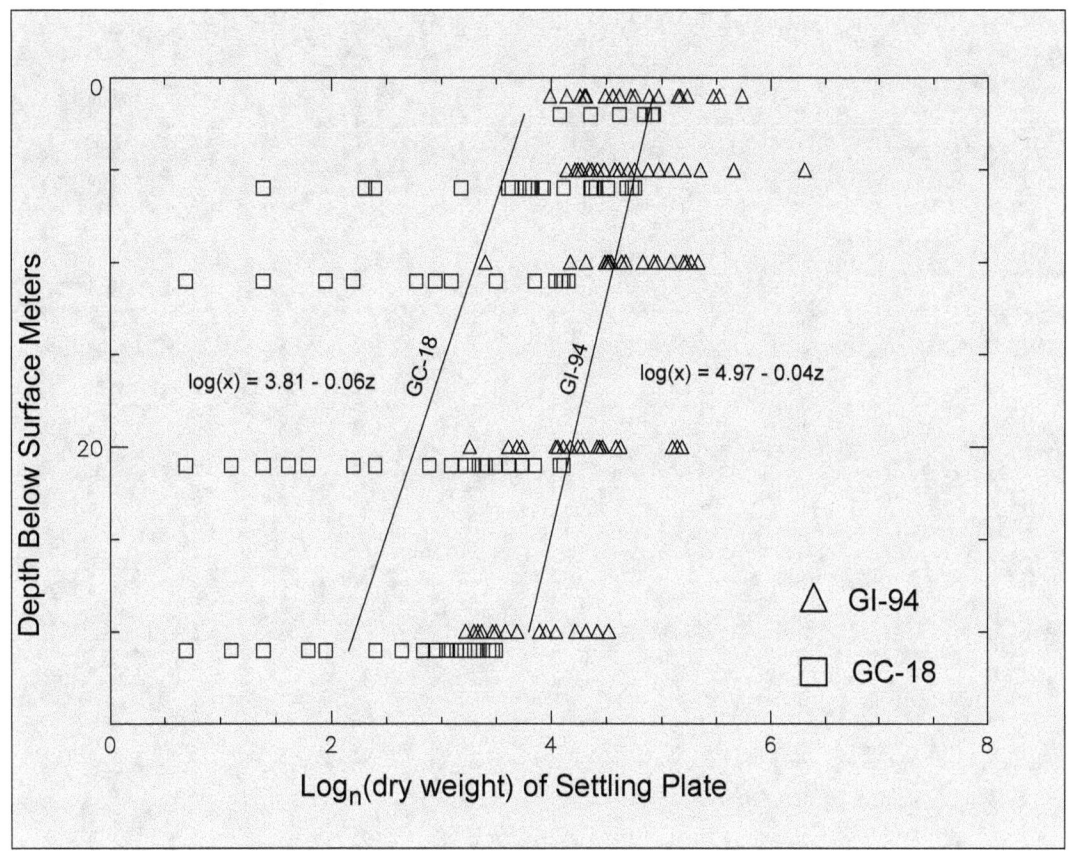

Figure 3.14. Settling plate dry weights regression against depth of deployment.

31

4 DISCUSSION

4.1 SCIENTIFIC FINDINGS

The results of the present study are generally consistent with previous works. ST-54 falls into the inshore assemblage group with a crust dominated by barnacles. GI-94 and GC-18 fall into the offshore assemblage as indicated by abundant bivalves. The outermost GC-18 does not conform to a bluewater assemblage. As reviewed previously, such an assemblage was not well established by Gallaway and Lewbel (1982). In spite of a considerable distance offshore surveyed by the Texas A&M University Corpus Christi group, a distinct bluewater assemblage has not been found (Dokken et al. 2000).

4.1.1 Biogeography and Platform Biotic Inventory

The present study along with the OEI investigation represent the easternmost survey of platform biota while ongoing studies by the Texas A&M Corpus Christi group and the Buccaneer Field study represent the westernmost. Similarity of results, allowing for different sampling methods, suggest that there is a common suite of carbonate-forming organisms across the region such that there are no major east-west biogeographic patterns other than the inshore/offshore change. The taxonomy of these species appears to be stable, although the autecology of the species has been poorly studied. Growth rates, reproduction timing, etc. are unknown. Assessment of mobile faunal is less complete. Although other reports list species names for the very abundant amphipods, there have been no contemporary revisions of the taxonomy of this extremely diverse group of organisms, and identification beyond genus may be questionable. Colonial and film-forming species are also problematic. There may be a common species pool across the region for algae, but hydroid and sponge taxonomy is too poorly developed to draw such conclusions. Expert taxonomic examination and possible revision must be conducted for the mobile and encrusting fauna before resolution of patterns can be made.

The only work east of the Mississippi has been Pequegnat and Pequegnat's (1968) settling study. That study produced a very different species inventory than surveys to the west of the river. Traditionally, the transition from heavily sedimented habitat west of the river to lower sedimentation habitat eastward has been considered a biogeographic boundary. A species change on offshore structures would be consistent with this view. Since scrape samples were not obtained, however, it is difficult to be confident about comparisons.

Overgrowing algae, hydroids, sponges, anemones, and corals show a similar strong contrast between inshore and offshore. Inshore, relatively thin (1 mm-5 mm) coverings of algae and hydroids cover the walls of the dense barnacle cover, but do not obscure the balanoids. Offshore, sponges are strongly dominant and can completely obscure the underlying barnacles and bivalves. Mobile fauna is dominated by amphipods and juvenile ophiuroids. Strong inshore versus offshore patterns were not obvious. These populations represent short-term phenomena with recruitment from the plankton.

This and previous studies have been descriptive and have undertaken no experimentation that can identify potential causes for the distinct inshore versus offshore zonation of cementing biota. Physiological stress brought about by lower salinity and colder winter temperatures inshore are obvious possibilities. The great abundance of the tree oyster *Isognomon bicolor* offshore is, however, hard to explain. *I. bicolor* is a mangrove prop root species well adapted to estuarine conditions. The possibility exists that the distinct inshore/offshore differences reflect competitive outcomes on these artificial systems different from outcomes on natural substrate.

The picture that emerges from comparison of substrate samples and mobile faunal samples is consistent with the apparent persistence of the fauna. Cementers showed distinct inshore/offshore patterns. Mobile invertebrates showed much less distinct zonation. Substrate formers are immobile (cemented) or virtually so (byssate). While we do not know the age of these organisms, size alone argues that they may be older than the much smaller mobile forms. Spatial pattern of substrate formers probably reflects a longer time integral of recruitment and long-term adult survival. Of the mobile fauna, amphipods are known to show short-term (possibly seasonal) fluctuation in abundance of several orders of magnitude (Beaver et al. 2003). As such, the patterns found reflect settlement and survival dynamics sampled at unknown stages in progression.

4.1.2 Depth Relationships

Depth changes have been noted by all authorities. Gallaway and Lewbel (1982) described a species and abundance shift, and Dokken et al. (2000) showed distinct vertical zonation in cluster analyses. Depth shifts found in this study differed among components. Shifts in species were noted in large-scale video survey, in scrapes of algae-containing overgrowth, and in apparent fouling rate of plates. They were not conspicuous in small-scale photography and scrapes of carbonate and mobile fauna. The differences may be due to sites, scales, and analytical methods. Both other studies include a greater range of depth. Both also scraped and photographed large areas on platforms. This may have the effect of sampling across faunal patches. The smaller samples of this study may have sampled within patches and missed larger-scale depth changes. Analytically, Gallaway and Lewbel (1982) did not employ similarity and cluster analysis. They depended upon abundance of select fauna to describe depth-associated changes. Dokken used Bray-Curtiss similarity and cluster analysis on composite data (images plus scrapes). The results showed such distinct depth zonation that the clustering algorithm may have been one that preserves sequences. Such methods are used in stratigraphy when zones are known to occur.

The strongest depth patterns were found in the settling-plate component. The significant negative correlation between depth and attached community dry weight is consistent with an exponential decrease in the rate of cover development with depth. Such decreases are expected in algae and algal-grazing fauna due to light attenuation. The pattern observed in this study is probably not light related, since the primary contribution to community dry weight is suspension-feeding barnacle and bryozoan tests. The depth decrease is most likely a function of decreasing food encounter. Two factors determine encounter rate, concentration of food particles and the flow rate of food-bearing water past the feeding structures. Neither of these was measured during the study, but depth decreases are reasonable for both. During summer months, extreme warming can produce sufficient temporary stratification to retain high plankton concentrations at the upper depths (1 and 5 m). Flow rate will be a function of orbital water movement under waves rather than currents for the depths of this study. This orbital flow decreases exponentially with depth.

4.1.3 Duration Relationship

Although the initial design included time-series sampling by all methods, such was only accomplished in the settling-plate component. Even in that component, unfortunately, inability to harvest plates according to a balanced design of depth and durations makes it difficult to confidently determine duration effects. At GI-94, weight versus duration showed no significant correlation ($r = -0.11$) over the 190 to 392 day experiments. At GC-18 the same correlation was significant ($r = -0.45$) over the 90 to 525 days of the experiment, but unexpectedly negative. The most valid conclusion that can be drawn is that duration and dry weight did not show a simple significant positive correlation. This was in spite of the simple supposition that colonization on a bare plate should increase with time in some manner. Aside from confounding of depth and duration effects, two ecological factors may be involved.

1. Initiation Dates—Colonization occurs when competent larvae encounter and accept the substrate. Plates deployed when larval conditions are optimal may be colonized immediately. Plates deployed long before optimal conditions may be colonized after a long wait. A collection of both types of plates will show a neutral or negative correlation between duration and degree of cover.

2. Grazing—The exposed flat surface of the settling plate offers far less refuge from predation than the adjacent rugose crust until a heavy cover is developed. One plate at GC-18 had two predatory snails (*Thais* sp.) foraging on its surface. Over a long period of time and over a large area, grazing and new recruitment should come into equilibrium such that cover is relatively stable and unrelated to additional duration of exposure. For small plates and short durations, the likelihood of predation without ensuing recolonization and compensation prior to plate harvest may be very high. Such predation would produce neutral to negative correlation with duration.

Resolution of date-of-initiation effects is possible in the future through extensive short-duration deployments, but may be logistically impractical. Grazing effects might be discerned and quantified through the use of caging experiments with appropriate controls. Development of exclusion systems that do not alter the small-scale hydrologic regime required by the settling larvae will, however, be a major challenge.

4.1.4   Production of Epibiotoic Crusts

Obtaining accurate and precise measurement of primary, secondary, and higher productivity at offshore platforms is a technically challenging task that was not attempted in this study. Population age/size relationships can be used to estimate overall population export (Beaver et al. 2003) under certain assumptions, but these methods are of no use for estimating production rates of colonial and film forming organisms. Considerable technique development remains to be undertaken. One finding of this study is that the accumulated weight of carbonate material may be a useful and simply obtained measure of net productivity over extended time intervals. Such measurements were obtained only in the settling-plate component.

A comparison between the settling plate results at GC-18 and GI-94 must be made cautiously due to the difference in duration experienced at both and the lack of replication at other platforms in the same general region. The two platforms do, however, appear to be developing crusts at different rates, the more offshore GC-18 slower than the more inshore. Three processes may be involved.

1. Larval Exposure—Plates at GI-94 tended to be heavily settled with barnacles and bryozoans. Plates at GC-18 were sparsely settled. While mortality between settlement and harvest is unknown, the possibility exists that GI-94 experienced greater exposure to competent larvae due to proximity of sources or local retention of water masses.

2. Water Column Productivity—High weights at GI-94 were associated with large barnacles and large bryozoan mats, indicating that post-settlement growth is an important factor. By contrast, barnacles and bryozoan patches at GC-18 were small. Indications are that filter feeders at GI-94 had a greater supply of food material in the adjacent water.

3. Grazing—The dry weight measurements used are standing stock and not actual production. It is possible that both platforms have similar production rates, but that greater predatory grazing at GC-18 produces the misleading appearance of limited production.

The settling plate findings that production at GC-18 is less, is in contrast with the visual impression of the platforms and the scrape sampling. Subjectively from video, both platforms seem to have similarly developed types and amounts of encrusting fauna. Cementing bivalves tended to form a base layer colonized by barnacles and tree oysters. The maximum dry weight of fouling was approximately $2.0g/cm^2$ found on a plate deployed at 5 m on GI-94 for 190 days. The plate was covered with a single to double layer of barnacles. Typical dry weights for this crust were 3.0 to $4.0g/cm^2$. If the crust production values at the two platforms are actually different, then the crust-forming organisms at GC-18 must be of greater average age.

4.1.5   Ecological Scenario: a Vertical Benthos

From the results reported here and a review of previous work, an ecological scenario can be developed that helps identify information needs. The over-riding characteristic of structure communities is that they are a vertical benthos deriving their primary small-scale habitat structure from biogenic carbonate crusts deposited by barnacles (balanoids), cementing bivalves (*Chama*, *Lopha*, etc.), and byssate bivalves (*Isognomon*, Arcidae, etc.). All of these foundation species are suspension feeders depending on the passing ocean water for nutrition. The extent of habitat development is limited by a balance between loss of shells and tests and new settlement plus growth. In a vertical benthos, shell material falls away rather than contributing to a growing carbonate base. Rather than reach a stable climax, platform communities are in a constant state of turnover. The mechanisms of loss can be proposed, but details and rates remain to be established. These include: predation, age-dependent mortality, competitive exclusion, bioerosion, corrosion of underlying metal, and wave surge.

The carbonate foundation species compete for space with adjacent individuals and with overgrowing colonial organisms (sponges, hydroids, anemones, bryozoans, etc.). Larger sponges and colonies of bryozoans deprive underlying organisms of food, killing them. These overgrowths are also suspension feeders depending on the surrounding ocean for food particles, but the small size for the feeding apparatus indicates a dependence on very small plankton, including bacteria. Collectively, they represent a different trophic route than the carbonate foundation species. The relative importance of macro, micro, and nanno filtration to overall platform production has not been determined. Similarly, the consumers of these overgrowths are poorly known.

Attached algae represent a special component of the platform system, since they are primary producers. As such, they fuel local food chains that can be independent of the surrounding plankton production. Rates of production and consumption by herbivores are very poorly known. During the course of this study, scanning electron micrographs of settlement plate surfaces revealed cleanly sheared algal stypes a fraction of a millimeter long (Shaughnessy, per com.). The observation that algae are abundant only on the top few meters of a platform may be misleading. Algal production may be high over the top several meters, but grazing is so intense that little biomass accumulates. The algal-based component of platform systems needs additional study.

In the present study large consumers of fouling organisms were limited to *Thais* (gastropod) and *Arbacia* (echinoid). Small consumers (amphipods, ophiuroids, and polychaetes) were abundant. The paucity of larger animals may simply reflect the realities of a vertical benthos; they eventually fall off. Smaller forms occupy the interstices of the carbonate matrix and are less likely to be lost. The trophic position of the small consumers is poorly known and largely unquantified. Specialized forms like pycnogonids feed hypodermically on hydrozoans. Amphipods are assumed to graze upon hydroids and possibly algae. Others may be part of a necrophagous/copraphagous food chain that feeds on biota killed by overgrowth and fecal material from the suspension feeders. The availability and persistence of a detrital resource must be strongly controlled by two factors, retention in the carbonate matrix versus flushing into the surrounding ocean by currents and surge.

The dynamics that cause more inshore platforms to be different than more offshore are essentially unknown. Oceanographic phenomena such as salinity, temperature, light attenuation, suspended material, etc. are highly likely to play important roles. Until the geography of the biotic transition is known, however, it is not possible to better assess what these roles might be. Biotic control remains a fully open question. Since the major plankton food source cannot be regulated by the platform community, important biotic interactions would most likely be (1) moderators of post-settlement competition and (2) moderators of crust loss. Predation, especially by fish, and bioerosion are processes that require detailed investigation. It is unlikely, however, that platforms ever become fully "reef-like" in the stable sense proposed by Bull and Kendall (1994). A climax will note be reached due to the unavoidable shedding of the carbonate crust in a vertical benthos will keep opening new patches for settlement from a frequently changing larval pool. Episodes and areas of biotic control may be quite transient.

4.1.6   Items for Future Investigation

From the present study and review of past work five high priority ecological questions can be posed about the artificial substrate communities in the Gulf of Mexico. These questions may not be management relevant in a strict sense, but they all contribute to the over riding question of what is the platform community doing? Answering these questions will be more important as the shift to fewer depth-spanning structures begins.

1. Habitat Equilibrium—What are the major processes of fouling community habitat accretion and destruction? At what rates do they proceed, and what determines the equilibrium condition across the northern Gulf of Mexico?

2. Trophic Structure—What is the overall quantitative primary and higher production on structures with special emphasis on routes to species of interest? Investigation should include suspension feeding, predation, necrophagy/copraphagy, and attached

algae. Development of effective methods is the primary limitation in obtaining an answer.

3. <u>Larger Geographic Pattern</u>—Do structures east of the Mississippi River draw from the same species pool as structures to the west? Aside from issues of taxonomic quality assurance, there are no restrictions on answering this question through additional survey.

4. <u>Better Resolution of Offshore Patterns</u>—Where does the transition from inshore to offshore communities occur along the coast, and with what oceanographic features does the shift coincide? Is there a distinct transition between offshore and bluewater communities at some region along the shelf? Both questions could be answered by means of additional surveying.

5. <u>Causes of Patterns</u>—What biotic and abiotic factors cause the shift from inshore to offshore communities? Answering this question will require autecological investigation of dominant species and innovative experimental manipulation.

4.2 UTILITY OF METHODS

This study employed a suite of methods that provided data on a range of spatial scales and taxonomic resolution. The following discussion and proposed design and logistics for future studies are based upon the experience gained.

4.2.1 Image-Based Methodology

Video and photographic methods are extremely appealing since they produce a very high data yield from the divers' time in the water. The results of this study have shown that video is an excellent means of conveying general information about a platform's biota, and that smaller-scale photography produces useful inventory data and illustration of patterns. The overall value of these methods, however, can best be judged in the context of a diving program that is time and personnel limited. Large amounts of time should not be devoted to video survey. In a large-scale survey, adequate video and high resolution photography can be undertaken as a lower level of activity. Video survey of a single leg suffices to capture major inter-platform differences. The value of high-resolution photography can be increased, if used in conjunction with scrape samples. The scrape site can be photographed before and after scraping and a series of images taken around the scrape to determine the spatial extent of the sampled biota.

4.2.2 Biota Sampling Methods

Biota were directly sampled by means of scraping and settlement plate recovery. The former sampled the time-integrated fouling crust, but with poor quantification. The latter are easily quantified, but sample only species that settle and survive until harvest. The scrape samples were the most informative with respect to overall community composition. In addition, the samples retained some spatial relationship among organisms. Supplemented with still images, scrape samples provide an excellent means of understanding overall system structure. This study did not attempt to assure consistent quantitative sampling. Pre-bagging of a scraped area as done by Fotheringham (1981) or use of a grab-like sampler (George and Thomas 1979) would improve quantification and retention of mobile fauna. These additions, however, will increase the time and effort needed to collect samples. In a large-scale survey, the benefits of a large number of samples versus fewer high-quality samples must be weighed.

Settling plate studies have been included in previous Gulf platform surveys, but the results have usually been presented as being secondary to scrape sampling except for Pequegnat and Pequegnat (1968). With respect to overall assessment of biota, scrape sampling alone suffices. Recruitment could also be determined from scrape samples, but with greater difficulty due to the complexity of the substrate. This study, settling plates provided two types of special information. First and most important, they showed dramatically that recruitment and fouling community developments rates are strongly depth dependent. Rate measurements cannot be obtained from scrapes. Second, they provided large samples of encrusting algae and bryozoans in a form more easily studied than in scrape samples.

This study followed the standard oceanographic procedure of bulk preservation with excess formalin (10%) in the field followed by water soaking and transfer to ethanol for long-term archival. This technique usually assures preservation, hardens tissues sufficiently to allow subsequent sectioning of organs, and eliminates specimen spoilage. Unfortunately, it makes small organisms too brittle for detailed examination of morphology, and it denatures DNA to a degree that hinders genetic studies. The hardening problem proved especially troublesome for algae, sponges, athecate hydroids, and athecate bryozoans. Although time demanding, future sampling should include more careful handling of exemplars, relaxation, and use of the taxa-specific preservation recommended by experts. DNA kits can be used in the field, or specimens dehydrated in absolute ethanol or deep frozen for molecular analysis.

4.2.3 Settling Plate System

The settling plate deployment was a qualified success that can be used in future studies with minor modification. Unless intentionally cut, as at GC-18, off-the-shelf ratchet cargo belts are strong enough to stay in place more than a year at and below 5 m. They are cheap, readily available, and light weight in air and water. Shallower, wave action is much greater and failure due to abrasion will be a problem with any fiber belt. Steel cable or chains must be used. Attachment of settling plates to the belt with heavy-duty cable ties was effective. Ties could be easily cut, and a plate replaced with little difficulty.

The most serious problem encountered was inability to deploy and recover plates according to the original design due to weather, operational constraints, and narrow windows of opportunity associated with working off the platforms. In order to be effective, sampling designs must make greater allowance for disruptions. A are minor problem was associated with record keeping. Each plate had a serial number engraved adjacent to one mounting hole. This made it simple to know what plate was being installed. On recovered plates, however, the number was usually obscured by fouling organisms. This required that a numbered tag be bagged in with each plate. The plate serial number could only be determined by scraping the organisms off during analysis. During this project, printed paper tags were used that did not stand up under preservation. In future studies, chemically resistant plastic tags should be used and affixed to each plate with a cable wrap by the diver.

The PVC plastic plates were colonized, but the question remains open as to how effective the surface is as a settlement substrate. The paucity of *Isognomon bicolor* and other bivalves common in scrape samples may indicate avoidance or loss during collection. Barnacles were strongly attached and usually left a basal plate when scraped off. Bryozoa, algae, and sponges, however, were easily scarped off the plates without residue. These forms may easily be dislodged in the field. Future studies might incorporate a variety of materials with effectiveness being evaluated via an analysis of variance.

4.3 LOGISTICS OF ANSWERING AND UNANSWERED QUESTIONS

In the 20+ years since Gallaway and Lewbel's synthesis of offshore platform ecology, age and geography of structures has changed appreciably. The fouling communities of old structures have matured, the density of structures across the shelf environment has increased, and rigid structures have been emplaced at depths of 1000 m beyond the edge of the shelf. As a result of increased stakeholder interest in fisheries issues, there has been considerable advancement in the sampling and description of fish populations associated with offshore structures (Stanley and Scarborough-Bull 2003 and references therein). Platform fish populations have been better surveyed (Rademacher and Render 2003), the zone of influence determined acoustically (Stanley and Wilson 2003), and early life histories considered (Hernandez et al. 2003). It has become increasingly apparent that the encrusted community interacts with the fish populations, providing food and habitat. The extent to which specific habitat types influence fish populations remains unknown, and the routes and rates of trophic transfer not directly measured.

Narrow management-related questions about the encrusting biota itself have arisen. Notably, to what extent do platforms serve as sources and stepping stones for alien species, and to what extent do platforms serve as extended habitat for desirable species and refuges from destructive trawling? The answers to all of these management-relevant questions can be incorporated into the framework of five ecological questions outlined in section 4.1.6. Clearly, some questions of biogeography can be answered now with wide-scale surveys and attention to taxonomic problems. Others that require rate measurements require technique development and testing. The experiences of this project provide suggestions for improved survey logistics.

4.3.1 Design and Logistics for a Large-Scale Survey

Based upon the utility of the various data types and the difficulty of SCUBA operations, the following mode of operation is suggested for future large-scale surveys. Experimental methods, such as settling plates and rate measurements, are omitted due to the need for additional development. A large-scale survey would sample along six shore to shelf break transects of 10 platforms (60 total) from south Texas to Alabama using oil and gas as well as navigation and communication structures.

1. Reconnaissance Digital Video—The primary use of digital video is to provide a quick and simple means of conveying the nature of each individual platform. Approximately one hour of footage along two vertical legs and representative horizontal members within 20 m of the surface is sufficient. Data-quality video requires for camera angle, distance to object, and lighting are too restrictive. Video is best used for illustration, not data.

2. Photo, Scrape, and Photo (PSP)—Photography (digital or film) will be most informative if directly combined with scrape sampling. A pre-scrape and post-scrape image will allow for reconstruction of position and quality control on scraping. Innovation is needed to improve scraping efficiency, retention, and quantification. In the absence of better techniques, simple manual scraping with quick bagging to capture mobile fauna is sufficient. An area of 25 cm x 35 cm should be adequate and practical.

3. Vessel-Based—Platform-based diving operations were used in this study for practical and fiscal reasons. It appears, however, that vessel-based operations afford a greater degree of operational flexibility. Unanticipated operational conflicts could be worked around, and a list of primary and contingency sites could be visited as needed.

4. 20 m and Above— Ideally, platforms should be surveyed from surface to bottom, but practical limits must be set. In the present study 99% of all taxa were collected within the top 20 m of water. Species composition continues to shifts a greater depths, but the overall species inventory remains relatively constant. Working deeper greatly decreases diver work time due both to additional swimming and to safely decompress.

5. Depth Strata—Sampling (PSP) should be stratified by depth. The current study's upper limit of 1 m was insufficient to sample the highly productive and diverse surface zone. Depths of 0, 1, 5, 10, 15, and 20 m should be sufficient. The shallowest will be most impacted by weather and surge. Greater depths can be surveyed by a special team at a few sites.

6. Replication—The current study found that both sampled legs were fairly similar as long as sampling is extensive enough to collect over biotic patches typically a meter or less in diameter. Therefore, a more informative large-scale survey design may increase the number of platforms visited by eliminating replicate sampling of legs within platforms. Within depth strata, however, replication of PSP samples should be as extensive as practical. Ten replicates should be taken at each depth at each site (60 samples per platform). Randomization of replicates could be accomplished by randomly marking a chain and wrapping it around the platform leg. Samples would be taken at marked points.

7. Teams—SCUBA sampling teams should consist of three divers. Two teams can work on the same platform leg simultaneously. A safety and sample-collecting boat with a driver and safety diver must be standing by. The overall dive team would consist of 8 people.

5 CONCLUSION

The algal-invertebrate growth sampled on offshore platforms ST-54, GI-94, and GC-18 are typical of biota found by previous studies in the same region and westward. The well-known barnacles and bivalves creating the main carbonate matrix of the crust are found from the mouth of the Mississippi westward to the limit of survey off Texas. Patterns eastward are unknown. The east-west pattern of less-known overgrowths of algae, sponges, and colonial forms is obscured by problems of species identification that can be resolved by a unified large-scale survey and better taxonomic quality assurance. The same is the case for small mobile fauna, such as highly abundant amphipods.

A distinct inshore-offshore change in fauna has been noted by all studies and was found here as well. Inshore platforms are dominated by dense populations of smaller barnacles covered with a relatively thin layer of algae and hydroids. Offshore platforms are dominated by a mix of cementing bivalves, byssate bivalves, and larger barnacles. This layer is overgrown and fatally smothered at places by sponges, hydroids, and bryozoa. The causes of the inshore-offshore zonation are unknown and a transition region has not been sampled. It is anticipated that carbonate-depositing forms reflect a longer integration of time than soft-tissue over growths and small mobile fauna. As such, barnacles and bivalves better reflect biogeographic processes, while the others have very high variances associated with short-term settlement and survival events.

For most species, there is little published information as to their preferred natural habitat. Therefore, it is not possible to assess their presence and role in fouling communities as "typical" or "unusual." There is one occurrence that appears to be "unusual", and there may be others. The tree oyster, *Isognomon bicolor*, is a byssate bivalve that forms numerous dense clusters on offshore platforms, but occurs only rarely inshore. Its natural habitat, however, is the prop roots of coastal mangroves, and its apparently greater success far offshore is unexplained. Biological interaction on platforms may be different than naturally encountered.

The entire fouling community is a continuously accreting and shedding system. Settlement is dependent upon the fluctuating larval supply in the surrounding water. The carbonate depositing fauna and soft-organism overgrowths are all dependent upon the surrounding water for food. Growth of the encrusting matrix is ultimately limited by destructive processes rather than food. Predation, competitive exclusion, and bioerosion directly remove crust or weaken it to the point that wave surge strips it off. The rates of crust formation and destruction are intertwined with trophic transfers within the fouling community and predator/grazing fish. Mechanisms of these processes are poorly understood and rates unknown.

This study employed common image-based and specimen-sampling methods of survey, in addition to experimental settling plate deployments. Each method yielded some useful information about the biota at each site. When funding and dive time are limited, however, certain activities are more informative for the cost and time involved. Video surveys are useful for illustration and developing an overall view of whole-platform ecology, but medium resolution seriously limits the quality of data that can be obtained. Photographs provided percent cover data and information about patterns of overgrowth, but failed to reveal the complexity of bivalve cover at the more offshore sites. Direct scrape samples provided the most complete data, but were not conducted in a manner that allowed quantification.

The only experiment attempted was the use of settling plates to determine the nature and rates of ongoing settlement. Unfortunately, the experiment proved too complex and demanding to be completed while dive opportunities were lost to weather and platform operations. The experiments did, however, show significant depth effects and inter-platform differences in development of a biofouling crust. Future use of settling plates should be considered in conjunction with other techniques for direct measurement of rate processes. Such techniques, unfortunately, require development.

The overall effectiveness of the project was negatively impacted by unanticipated problems associated with carrying out time-series studies from platforms. The GC-18 and ST-54 platforms initiated major drilling or re-drilling during the study, greatly restricting diving opportunities. The effectiveness of future studies may be improved by basing diving operations on research vessels and designing contingency surveys that target more than one candidate structure in ocean areas of interest.

6 LITERATURE CITED

Abbott, T. 1953. American Seashells. D. Van Nostrand Co. New York. 542 pp.

Andrew, N.L. and B.D. Mapstone. 1987. Sampling and the description of spatial pattern in marine ecology. In: M. Barnes (ed.) Oceanography and Marine Biology Progress Series 25:39-90.

Aronson, R.B., P.J. Edmunds, W.F. Precht, D.W. Swanson, and D.R. Levitan. 1994. Large scale, long-term monitoring of Caribbean coral reefs: simple, quick, inexpensive techniques. Atoll Research Bulletin 421:1-19.

Beaver, C., S. Childs, and Q. Dokken. 2003. Secondary productivity within biotic fouling community elements on two artificial reef structures in the northwestern Gulf of Mexico. American Fisheries Society Symposium 36:195-204.

Bedinger, C.A., Jr. and L.Z. Kirby (eds.) 1981. Ecological investigations of petroleum production platforms in the central Gulf of Mexico. Southwest Research Institute Project 01-5245. U.S. Dept. of the Interior, Bureau of Land Management, New Orleans, La. 199 pp.

Bohnsack, J.A. and S.P. Bannerot. 1986. A stationary visual census technique for quantitatively assessing community structure of coral reef fishes. U.S. Dept. of Commerce, NOAA Tech. Rep. NMFS 41, 15 pp.

Bohnsack, J.A. 1979. Photographic quantitative sampling of hard-bottom benthic communities. Bulletin of Marine Science 29:242-252.

Bull, A.S. and J.J. Kendall, Jr. 1994. An indication of the process: Offshore platforms as artificial reefs in the Gulf of Mexico. Bulletin Marine Science 55:1086-1098.

Bert, T.M. and H.J. Humm. 1979. Checklist of the marine algae on the offshore oil platforms of Louisiana. In: C.H. Ward, M.E. Bender, and D.J. Reish (eds.). The offshore ecology investigation: Effects of oil drilling and production in a coastal environment. Rice University Studies 65:437-446.

Butman, C.A., J.P. Grassle, and C.M. Webb. 1988. Substrate choices made by marine larvae settling in still water and flume flow. Nature 333:771-773.

Canu, F. and R.S. Bassler. 1928. Fossil and recent bryozoa of the Gulf of Mexico region. Proceedings of the United States National Museum, 72:1-199.

Carlton, J.H. and T. Done. 1995. Quantitative video sampling of coral reef benthos: Large-scale application. Coral Reefs 14:35-46.

Carney, R.S. 1987. A review of study designs for the detection of long-term environmental effects of offshore petroleum activities. In: D.F. Boesch and N.N. Rabalais (eds.). Long-term environmental effects of offshore oil and gas development. New York: Elsevier.

Chayes, F. 1956. Petrographic Modal Analysis. New York: John Wiley & Sons. 113 pp.

Coan, E., P.V. Scott, and F. R. Bernard. 2000. Bivalve seashells of western North America. Santa Barbara Museum of Natural History, Santa Barbara, Calif. 764 pp.

Connell, J.H. 1961. The influence of interspecific competition and other factors on the distribution of the barnacle *Chthamalus stellatus*. Ecology 42:710-723.

Dayton, P.K. 1971. Competition, disturbance and community organization: The provision and subsequent utilization of space in a rocky intertidal community. Ecological Monograph 41:351-389.

Dodge, R.E., A. Logan, and A. Antonius. 1982. Quantitative reef assessment studies in Bermuda: A comparison of methods and preliminary results. Bulletin of Marine Science 32:745-760.

Dokken, Q.R., K. Withers, S. Childs, and T. Riggs. 2000. Characterization and comparison of platform reef communities off the Texas coast. Prepared for Texas Parks and Wildlife Department. Texas A&M University Corpus Christi. TAMU-CC-0007-CCS. 75 pp.

Edgerton, H. 1983.Electronic flash and strobe. Cambridge, Mass.: MIT Press.

Evans, S.M. 1999. Tributyltin pollution: the catastrophe that never happened. Marine Pollution Bulletin 38:629-636.

Foster, B.A. and R.C. Willan. 1979. Foreign barnacles transported to New Zealand on an oil platform. New Zealand Journal of Marine & Freshwater Research 13:143-149.

Fotheringham, N. 1981. Observations on the effects of oil field structures on their biotic environment. In: B.S. Middleditch (ed.). Environmental effects of offshore oil production. The Buccaneer Gas and Oil Field Study. Marine Science 14:179-206.

Fucik, K.W. and I.T. Show. 1981. Environmental synthesis using an ecosystems model. In: B.S. Middleditch (ed.). Environmental effects of offshore oil production: The Buccaneer Gas and Oil Field Study. Marine Science 14:329-354.

Gallaway, B.J., L.R. Martin, R.L. Howard, G.S. Boland, and G.S. Dennis. 1981a. In: B.S. Middleditch (ed.). Environmental effects of offshore oil production. The Buccaneer Gas and Oil Field Study. Marine Science 14:237-299.

Gallaway, B.J., M.F. Johnson, L.R. Martin, F.J. Margraf, G.S. Lewbel, R.L. Howard, and G.S. Boland. 1981b. The artificial reef studies. In: C.A. Bedinger, Jr. and L.Z. Kirby (eds.). Ecological investigations of petroleum production platforms in the central Gulf of Mexico. Southwest Research Institute Project 01-5245. U.S. Dept. of the Interior, Bureau of Land Management, New Orleans, La. 199 pp.

Gallaway, B. and G. Lewbel. 1982. The ecology of petroleum platforms in the northwestern Gulf of Mexico: A community profile. U.S. Dept. of the Interior, Fish and Wildlife Service, Biological Services Program FWS/OBS-82/72, BLM Open File Report 82-03. 52 pp.

George, R.Y. and P.J. Thomas 1979. Biofouling community dynamics in Louisiana shelf oil platforms in the Gulf of Mexico. In: C.H. Ward, M.E. Bender, and D.J. Reish (eds.). The offshore ecology investigation: effects of oil drilling and production in a coastal environment. Rice Univ. Studies 65:553-574.

Gittings, S.R., G.D. Dennis, and H.W. Harry. 1986. Annotated guide to the barnacles of the northern Gulf of Mexico. Texas Sea Grant Publication 86-402. NA85AA-D-SG128. 36 pp.

Gunter, G. and R.A. Geyer. 1955. Studies on the fouling organisms of the northwest Gulf of Mexico. Publications Institute Marine Science Univ. Texas 4(1):37-87.

Hernandez, F.J., R.F. Shaw, J.S. Cope, J.G. Ditty, T. Farooqi, and M.C. Benfield. 2003. The across-shelf larval, postlarval, and juvenile fish assemblages collected at offshore oil and gas platforms west of the Mississippi River Delta. American Fisheries Society Symposium 36:39-72.

Hooper, J.N.A. and Wiedenmayer, F. 1994. Porifera. In: Wells, A. (ed.). Zoological Catalogue of Australia. Canberra, Australia: AGPS. 12:1-621.

Hooper, J.N.A. 2000. 'SPONGUIDE'. Guide to sponge collection and identification. www.qmuseum.qld.gov.au/organisation/sections/SessileMarineInvertebrates/spong.pdf

Hooper, J.N.A. and R.W.M. Van Soest (eds.). 2003. Systema porifera: A guide to the classification of sponges. New York: Plenum. 2 vols. 1804 pp.

Keenan, S.F., M.C. Benfield, and R.F. Shaw. 2003. Zooplanktivory by blue runner *Caranx crysos*: A potential energetic subsidy to Gulf of Mexico fish populations at petroleum platforms. American Fisheries Society Symposium 36:167-180.

Laughton, A.S. 1959. Photography of the seafloor. Endeavor 18:178-185.

Littler, D.S. and M.M. Littler. 2000. Caribbean reef plants. Washington, DC: Offshore Graphics. 542 pp.

Loya, Y. 1978. Community structure and species diversity of hermatypic corals at Eilat, Red Sea. Marine Biology 13:100-123.

MacArthur, R.H. 1972. Geographical ecology. New York: Harper and Rowe. 269 pp.

MacArthur, R.H. and E.O. Wilson. 1967. The theory of island biogeography. Princeton: Princeton University Press. 203 pp.

Maki, J.S., A.B. Yule, D. Rittschof, and R. Mitchell. 1994. The effect of bacterial films on the temporary adhesion and permanent fixation of cypris larvae, *Balanus amphitrite* Darwin. Biofouling 8:121-131.

Marsden, J.E. and D. M. Lansky. 2000. Substrate selection by settling zebra mussels, *Dreissena polymorpha*, relative to material, texture, orientation, and sunlight. Canadian Journal Zoology 78:787-793.

McGrail, D.W. and M. Carnes. 1983. Shelfedge dynamics and the nephloid layer in the northwestern Gulf of Mexico. In: J.D. Stanley and G.T. Moore (ed.). Shelf break: Critical interface on continental margins. Society Economic Paleontology Mineralogy Special Publication 33:215-264.

Middleditch, B.S. (ed.) 1981. Environmental effects of offshore oil production: The Buccaneer gas and oil field study. Marine Science 14:1-446.

Mitchell, R. and D. Kirchman. 1984. The microbial ecology of marine surfaces. In: *Marine* and metamorphosis in the marine environment. In: Costlow, J.D. and R.C. Tipper (eds.). Marine biodeterioration: Advanced biodeterioration: An interdisciplinary study. Annapolis, Md: Naval Institute Press. Pp. 49-56.

Paine, R.T. 1974. Intertidal community structure. Experimental studies on the relationship between dominant competitor and its principal predator. Oecologia 15:93-120.

Pequegnat, W.E. and L.H. Pequegnat. 1968. Ecological aspects of marine fouling in the northeastern Gulf of Mexico. Final report to the U.S. Dept. of Defense, Office of Naval Research, Navy Department Project NR 083-036. 80 pp.

Pineda, J. 1994. Spatial and temporal patterns in barnacle settlement rate along a southern California rocky shore. Marine Ecology Progress Series 107:125-138.

Pitcher, T.J., and W. Seaman, Jr. 2000. Petrarch's principle: how protected human-made reefs can help the reconstruction of fisheries and marine ecosystems. Fish and Fisheries 1:73-81.

Rabalais, N.N., M.J. Dagg, and D.F. Boesch. 1985. Nationwide review of oxygen depletion and eutrophication in estuaries and coastal waters: Gulf of Mexico (Alabama, Mississippi, Louisiana, and Texas). Final report to the U.S. Dept. of Commerce, National Oceanic and Atmospheric Agency, Rockville, Md.

Rademacher, K.R. and J.H. Render. 2003. Fish assemblages around oil and gas platforms n the northeastern Gulf of Mexico: Developing a survey design. American Fisheries Society Symposium 36:101-122.

Rogers, C., G. Garrison, R. Gober, Z.M. Hillis, and M.A. Frank. 1994. Coral reef monitoring manual for the Caribbean and Western Atlantic. U.S. Dept. of the Interior, National Park Service. 100 pp.

Schneider, C.W. and R.B. Searles. 1991. Seaweeds of the southeastern United States: Cape Hatteras to Cape Canaveral. Durham and London:Duke University Press. 553 pp.

Schoener, A. 1974. Experimental zoogeography: Colonization of marine mini-islands. American Naturalist 108:715-139.

Smith, S.D.A. and M.J. Rule. 2002. Artificial substrata in a shallow sublittoral habitat: Do they adequately represent natural habitats or the local species pool? J. Exp. Marine Biology and Ecology 277:25-41.

Stanley, D.R. and A. Scarborough-Bull (eds.). 2003. Fisheries, reefs, and offshore development. American Fisheries Society Symposium 36. Proceedings of the Gulf of Mexico Fish and Fisheries Meeting held at New Orleans, La. 24-26 October 2000. Bethesda Md:American Fisheries Soc. 238 pp.

Stanley, D.R. and C.A. Wilson. 2003. Seasonal and spatial variation in the biomass and size frequency distribution of fish associated with oil and gas platforms in the northern Gulf of Mexico. American Fisheries Society Symposium 36:123-154.

Stanley, D.R. and C.A. Wilson. 1997. Seasonal and spatial variation in abundance and size distribution of fishes associated with petroleum platforms in the northern Gulf of Mexico. Canadian Journal of Fisheries and Aquatic Sciences 54:1166-1176.

Stanley, D.R. and C.A. Wilson. 1996. The use of hydroacoustics to determine abundance and size distribution of fishes associated with a petroleum platform. International Council on the Exploration of the Sea. Journal of Marine Science 53:473-477.

Steinberg, P.D., R. de Nys, and S. Kjelleberg. 2001. Chemical mediation of surface colonization: Chapter 10. In: J.B. McClintock and B.J. Baker (eds.). Marine Chemical Ecology, Boca Raton, Fla.: CRC Press.

Sutherland, J.P. and R. Karlson. 1977. Development and stability of the fouling community at Beaufort North Carolina. Ecological Monographs 47:425-446.

Tolan, J. 2001. Patterns of reef-fish larval supply to petroleum platforms in the northern Gulf of Mexico. Ph.D. dissertation, Louisiana State University, Baton Rouge. 194 pp.

van der Plas, L. and A.C. Tobi. 1965. A chart for judging the reliability of point counting results. American Journal of Science 263:87-90.

Vevers, H.G. 1951. Photography of the sea floor. Journal Marine Biological Association of the United Kingdom 30:101-111.

Ward, C.H., M.E. Bender, and D.J. Reish. 1979. The offshore ecology investigation: Effects of oil drilling and production in a coastal environment. Rice University Studies. Vol 65, 589 pp.

Woods Hole Oceanographic Institution. 1952. Marine fouling and its prevention. Prepared for the Navy Department Bureau of Ships, United States Naval Institute, Annapolis, Md. 388 pp.

APPENDIX A

CHECKLIST OF ALGAE SPECIES

Compiled by Frank Shaunagessy, Humbolt State University

Reference specimens are maintained at the LSU Herbarium.

Because the majority of algal literature for the northern Gulf of Mexico is 25-35 years old, it is currently not possible to contrast the Louisiana algal flora, or specifically platform algal communities, to any of the better studied algal floras along the southeast states and Caribbean. Being able to make reliable floral comparisons among geographic locations is an important first step in understanding where platform algae are being dispersed from and the abiotic and biotic processes that are likely to be important to platform ecosystems. Thus, we used more recent floral treatments by Schneider and Searles (1991) and Wynne (1986) from the southeast states and the Atlantic western tropics in order to update specific epithets from the Louisiana literature. Dawes (1974) is the taxonomic reference for the cyanobacteria as he provides useful drawings and black/white photographs. Most studies used to produce this list of updated names are only from Louisiana but one study (Eiseman and Blair 1982) extends to the Louisiana/Texas border at the Flower Gardens and another study (Earle 1969; subregion A) covers eastern Louisiana to mid Alabama. The algae listed by Bert and Humm (1979) from eight Louisiana oil platforms on an east/west transect is also included as well as taxa identified to date in the present study which samples platforms on a north/ south transect.

Taxa

Cyanophyta
Chroococcales
Chroococcaceae

Agmenellum thermale (Kützing) Drouand and Daily
    Taxonomic reference: **Dawes (1974)**
    Cited in the following Louisiana studies: Humm and Darnell (1959), Bert and Humm (1979), Humm and Bert (1979)

Anacystis aeruginosa (Zanardini) Drouand and Daily
    Taxonomic reference: **Dawes (1974)**
    Cited in the following Louisiana studies: Humm and Caylor (1957), Bert and Humm (1979), Humm and Bert (1979)

Anacystis dimidiata (Kützing) Drouand and Daily
    Taxonomic reference: **Dawes (1974)**
    Cited in the following Louisiana studies: Humm and Caylor (1957), Bert and Humm (1979), Humm and Bert (1979)

Anacystis marina (Hansgirg) Drouet and Daily
    Cited in the following Louisiana studies: Humm and Caylor (1957), Humm and Bert (1979)

Anacystix montona (Lightfoot) Drouand and Dailey
    Taxonomic reference: **Dawes (1974)**
    Cited in the following Louisiana studies: Bert and Humm (1979), Humm and Bert (1979)

Coccochloris elabens (Brébisson) Drouand and Daily
    Taxonomic reference: **Dawes (1974)**
    Cited in the following Louisiana studies: Bert and Humm (1979), Humm and Bert (1979)

Coccochloris stagnina Drouet and Daily
    Cited in the following Louisiana studies: Bert and Humm (1979), Humm and Bert (1979)

Entophysalis conferta (Kützing) Drouand and Dailey
    Taxonomic reference: **Dawes (1974)**

Cited in the following Louisiana studies: Humm and Caylor (1957), Bert and Humm (1979), Humm and Bert (1979), present study

Entophysalis deusta (Meneghini) Drouand and Daily
Taxonomic reference: **Dawes (1974)**
Cited in the following Louisiana studies: Humm and Caylor (1957), Bert and Humm (1979), Humm and Bert (1979)

Gomphosphaeria aponina Kützing
Taxonomic reference: **Dawes (1974)**
Cited in the following Louisiana studies: Humm and Bert (1979)

Johannesbaptistia pellucida Taylor and Drouand
Taxonomic reference: **Dawes (1974)**
Cited in the following Louisiana studies: Bert and Humm (1979), Humm and Bert (1979)

Nostocales
Oscillatoriaceae

Microcoleus chthonoplastes (Flora Danica) Thurand
Cited in the following Louisiana studies: Humm and Caylor (1957)

Microcoleus lyngbyaceus (Kützing) Crouan
Taxonomic reference: **Dawes (1974)**
Cited in the following Louisiana studies: Bert and Humm (1979), Humm and Bert (1979)
Synonyms from Louisiana studies: as *Lyngbya confervoides, Lyngbya semiplena, Lyngbya aestuarii, Hydrocoleum lyngbyaceum* by Humm and Caylor (1957); as *Lyngbya majuscula* by Humm and Darnell (1959), present study

Microcoleus vaginatus (Vaucher) Gomont
Taxonomic reference: **Dawes (1974)**
Cited in the following Louisiana studies: Bert and Humm (1979), Humm and Bert (1979)

Oscillatoria erythraea (Ehrenberg) Kützing
Taxonomic reference: **Dawes (1974)**
Cited in the following Louisiana studies: Bert and Humm (1979)
Synonyms from Louisiana studies: as *Trichodesmium thiebautii* by Humm and Caylor (1957), Humm and Bert (1979)

Oscillatoria lutea Agardh
Taxonomic reference: **Dawes (1974)**
Cited in the following Louisiana studies: Bert and Humm (1979)
Synonyms from Louisiana studies: as *Lyngbya lutea* by Humm and Caylor (1957), Humm and Bert (1979)

Oscillatoria subuliformis (Thwaites) Gomont
Cited in the following Louisiana studies: Humm and Caylor (1957)

Phormidium submembranaceum (Ardissone and Strafforello) Gomont
Cited in the following Louisiana studies: Humm and Caylor (1957)
Synonyms from Louisiana studies: as *Oscillatoria submembranacea*
Ardissone and Strafforello by Bert and Humm (1979), Humm and Bert (1979)

Plectonema nostocorum Borand
Cited in the following Louisiana studies: Humm and Caylor (1957)

Plectonema terebrans Bornand and Flahault
    Cited in the following Louisiana studies: Humm and Caylor (1957)

Porphyrosiphon kurzii (Zeller) Drouet
    Cited in the following Louisiana studies: Humm and Bert (1979)

Porphyrosiphon notarisii (Meneghini) Kützing
    Taxonomic reference: **Dawes (1974)**
    Cited in the following Louisiana studies: Bert and Humm (1979), Humm and Bert (1979)
    Synonyms from Louisiana studies: as *Oscillatoria nigro-viridis* by Humm and Caylor (1957), present
    study

Schizothrix arenaria (Berkeley) Gomont
    Taxonomic reference: **Dawes (1974)**
    Cited in the following Louisiana studies: Bert and Humm (1979), Humm and Bert (1979)
    Synonyms from Louisiana studies: as *Microcoleus tenerrimus* by Humm and Caylor (1957), as
    Schizothrix tenerrima by Bert and Humm (1979) and Humm and Bert (1979)
    Note: *S. tennerrima* is not listed as a synonym of *S. arenaria* by Dawes (1974) but, given the use of
    'tenerrimus', we are treating *S. tenrrima* as a synonym of *S. arenaria.*

Schizothrix calcicola (Agardh) Gomont
    Taxonomic reference: **Dawes (1974)**
    Cited in the following Louisiana studies: Bert and Humm (1979), Humm and Bert (1979)
    Synonyms from Louisiana studies: as *Lyngbya epiphytica* by Humm and Caylor (1957), present
    study

Schizothrix mexicana Gomont
    Taxonomic reference: **Dawes (1974)**
    Cited in the following Louisiana studies: Bert and Humm (1979), Humm and Bert (1979)
    Synonyms from Louisiana studies: as *Lyngbya gracilis* by Humm and Darnell (1959), present study

Spirulina subsalsa Oersted
    Taxonomic reference: **Dawes (1974)**
    Cited in the following Louisiana studies: Humm and Darnell (1959), Bert and Humm (1979), Humm
    and Bert (1979)
    Synonyms from Louisiana studies: as *Spirulina major* by Humm and Caylor (1957), present study

Symploca atlantica Gomont
    Taxonomic reference: this species is not mentioned by Dawes but all species of *Symploca* cited by
    Dawes are considered synonyms of *Schizothrix arenaria.*
    Cited in the following Louisiana studies: Humm and Caylor (1957)

Nostocaceae

Nodularia harveyana (Thwaites) Thurand
    Taxonomic reference: **Dawes (1974)**
    Cited in the following Louisiana studies: Humm and Caylor (1957)

Nodularia spumigena Mertens var. *major* (Kützing) Bornet and Flahault
    Taxonomic reference: **Dawes (1974)**
    Synonyms from Louisiana studies: as *Nostoc spumigena* by Humm and Bert (1979)
    Note: *Nostoc spumigena* (Mertens) Drouet is not synonomized into *N. spumigena* by Dawes but,
    given that the species name and authority are the same, we are treating *N. spumigena* as being
    synonymous with *N. spumigena.*

A-5

Stigonemataceae

Amphithrix violecea (Kützing) Bornet and Flahault
Taxonomic reference: genus and species not mentioned by Dawes
Cited in the following Louisiana studies: Humm and Caylor (1957)

Mastigcoleus testarum Lagerheim
Taxonomic reference: **Dawes (1974)**
Cited in the following Louisiana studies: Humm and Caylor (1957), Bert and Humm (1979), Humm and Bert (1979)

Rivulariaceae

Calothrix confervicola (Roth) C. Agardh
Taxonomic reference: **Dawes (1974)**
Cited in the following Louisiana studies: Humm and Caylor (1957), present study

Calothrix crustacea Thuret
Taxonomic reference: **Dawes (1974)**
Cited in the following Louisiana studies: Humm and Caylor (1957), Bert and Humm (1979), Humm and Bert (1979), present study

Chlorophyta
Tetrasporales

Pseudotetraspora marina Wille
Taxonomic reference: **Wynne (1986)**, genus and species not included in Schneider and Searles (1991)
Synonyms from Louisiana studies: as *Pseudotetraspora antillarum* by Bert and Humm (1979), Humm and Bert (1979)

Ulotrichales
Ulotrichaceae

Gomontia polyrhiza (Langerheim) Bornand and Flahault
Taxonomic reference: **Schneider and Searles (1991), Wynne (1986)**
Cited in the following Louisiana studies: Bert and Humm (1979), Humm and Bert (1979)

Monostroma oxyspermum (Kützing) Doty
Taxonomic reference: **Schneider and Searles (1991)**, not in Wynne (1986)
Cited in the following Louisiana studies: Humm and Bert (1979)

Ulothrix flacca (Dillwyn) Thuret
Taxonomic reference: **Schneider and Searles (1991), Wynne (1986)**
Cited in the following Louisiana studies: Humm and Bert (1979), Kapraun (1974)

Ulvales
Ulvellaceae

Entocladia viridis Reinke
> Taxonomic reference: **Schneider and Searles (1991)**; as *Acrochaete viridis* in Wynne (1986)
> Cited in the following Louisiana studies: Humm and Caylor (1957), Bert and Humm (1979)

Epicladia testarum (Kylin) R. Nielsen
> Taxonomic reference: **Wynne (1986), Edwards (1976)**
> Synonyms from Louisiana studies: as *Entocladia testarum* Kapraun (1974), present study

Phaeophila dendroides (Crouan) Batters
> Taxonomic reference: **Schneider and Searles (1991), Wynne (1986)**
> Cited in the following Louisiana studies: Humm and Darnell (1959), Bert and Humm (1979), Kapraun (1974)

Phaeophila floridearum Hauck
> Taxonomic reference: species not mentioned by either Schneider and Searles (1991) or Wynne (1986) or Dawes (1974)
> Cited in the following Louisiana studies: Humm and Caylor (1957)

Pseudoclonium marinum (Reinke) Alleem and Schulz
> Taxonomic reference: **Wynne (1986), Dawes (1974)**, questionable record of the genus noted in Schneider and Searles (1991)
> Cited in the following Louisiana studies: Humm and Bert (1979), as *Protoderma marinum* by Bert and Humm (1979)
> Note: Kapraun (1974) lists a species within this genus from Louisiana as '*P. submarinum*'. Based on examination of the species lists above, we consider '*submarinum*' to be an orthographic variant of *marinum*..

Stichococcus marinus (Wille) Hazen
> Taxonomic reference: **Wynne (1986)**, not mentioned in Schneider and Searles (1991)
> Cited in the following Louisiana studies: Humm and Caylor (1957), Bert and Humm (1979), Humm and Bert (1979)

Ulvella lens Crouan
> Taxonomic reference: **Schneider and Searles (1991), Wynne (1986)**
> Cited in the following Louisiana studies: Humm and Caylor (1957), Humm and Darnell (1959), Bert and Humm (1979), Humm and Bert (1979), Kapraun (1974)

Ulvaceae

Blidingia marginata (J. Agardh) P. Dangeard
> Taxonomic reference: **Schneider and Searles (1991), Wynne (1986)**
> Cited in the following Louisiana studies: Kapraun (1974)

Blidingia minima (Kützing) Kylin
> Taxonomic reference: **Schneider and Searles (1991), Wynne (1986)**
> Cited in the following Louisiana studies: Kapraun (1974)

Enteromorpha clathrata (Roth) J. Agardh
> Taxonomic reference: **Schneider and Searles (1991), Wynne (1986)**
> Cited in the following Louisiana studies: Humm and Darnell (1959), Bert and Humm (1979), Humm and Bert (1979), Mullahy (1959), Kapraun (1974)

Enteromorpha compressa (L.) Nees
    Taxonomic reference: **Schneider and Searles (1991)**, as *E. compressa* (L.) Greville in Wynne (1986), Dawes (1974)
    Cited in the following Louisiana studies: Bert and Humm (1979), Humm and Bert (1979)

Enteromorpha flexuosa J. Agardh
    Taxonomic reference: **Schneider and Searles (1991),** and **Wynne (1986)** with ssp. *forma*
    Cited in the following Louisiana studies: Humm and Caylor (1957), Bert and Humm (1979), Humm and Bert (1979), Mullahy (1959), Kapraun (1974)
    Synonyms from Louisiana studies: as *Enteromorpha lingulata, Enteromorpha plumosa* by Humm and Caylor (1957), Bert and Humm (1979), Humm and Bert (1979), Mullahy (1959), Kapraun (1974), as *Enteromorpha erecta* by Bert and Humm (1979), Humm and Bert (1979)

Enteromorpha intestinalis (L.) Nees
    Taxonomic reference: **Schneider and Searles (1991)**, as *E. intestinalis* (L.) Link in Wynne (1986)
    Cited in the following Louisiana studies: Bert and Humm (1979), Humm and Bert (1979)

Enteromorpha linza (L.) J. Agardh
    Taxonomic reference: **Schneider and Searles (1991)**, **Wynne (1986)**
    Cited in the following Louisiana studies: Kapraun (1974), present study

Enteromorpha prolifera (O.F. Muller) J. Agardh
    Taxonomic reference: **Schneider and Searles (1991)**, **Wynne (1986)**
    Cited in the following Louisiana studies: Bert and Humm (1979), Humm and Bert (1979), as *E. salina* by Bert and Humm (1979) and Humm and Bert (1979), Kapraun (1974)

Enteromorpha ramulosa (J.E. Smith) Carmichael
    Taxonomic reference: **Schneider and Searles (1991)**, **Wynne (1986)**
    Cited in the following Louisiana studies: Kapraun (1974)

Ulva curvata (Kützing) De Toni
    Taxonomic reference: **Schneider and Searles (1991)**, **Wynne (1986)**
    Cited in the following Louisiana studies: Humm and Bert (1979)

Ulva rigida C. Agardh
    Taxonomic reference: **Schneider and Searles (1991)**, **Wynne (1986)**
    Synonyms from Louisiana studies: as *Ulva lactuca* by Humm and Caylor (1957), Eiseman and Blair 1982, Mullahy (1959), Kapraun (1974)

Cladophorales
Anadyomenaceae

Anadyomene stellata (Wulfen) C. Agardh
    Taxonomic reference: **Wynne (1986),** species not in Schneider and Searles (1991)
    Cited in the following Louisiana studies: Eiseman and Blair (1982)

Microdictyon boergesenii Sandchell
    Taxonomic reference: **Schneider and Searles (1991)**, **Wynne (1986)**
    Cited in the following Louisiana studies: Eiseman and Blair (1982)

Boodleaceae

Struvea sp.
Taxonomic reference: **Schneider and Searles (1991), Wynne (1986)**
Cited in the following Louisiana studies: Eiseman and Blair (1982)

Cladophoraceae

Chaetomorpha brachygona Harvey
Taxonomic reference: **Schneider and Searles (1991), Wynne (1986)**
Cited in the following Louisiana studies: Bert and Humm (1979), Humm and Bert (1979)

Chaetomorpha gracilis Kützing
Taxonomic reference: **Schneider and Searles (1991), Wynne (1986)**
Cited in the following Louisiana studies: Bert and Humm (1979)

Chaetomorpha linum (O.F. Müller) Kützing
Taxonomic reference: **Schneider and Searles (1991), Wynne (1986)**
Cited in the following Louisiana studies: Bert and Humm (1979), Humm and Bert (1979), Kapraun (1974)

Chaetomorpha minima Collins and Hervey
Taxonomic reference: **Schneider and Searles (1991), Wynne (1986)**
Cited in the following Louisiana studies: Bert and Humm (1979), Humm and Bert (1979)

Cladophora albida (Nees) Kützing
Taxonomic reference: **Schneider and Searles (1991)**
Cited in northern Gulf flora by: Bert and Humm (1979)
Note: Schneider and Searles (1991) cite one study from the southeastern states where *C. albida* was misidentified as *Cladophora delicatula*.

Cladophora catenata (L.) Kützing
Taxonomic reference: **Wynne (1986)**, species not included in Schneider and Searles (1991)
Cited in the following Louisiana studies: Bert and Humm (1979)

Cladophora coelothirx Kützing
Taxonomic reference: **Wynne (1986)**, species not included in Schneider and Searles (1991)
Synonyms from Louisiana studies: as *Cladophora repens* by Bert and Humm (1979), Kapraun (1974)

Cladophora dalmatica Kützing
Taxonomic reference: **Schneider and Searles (1991), Wynne (1986)**
Cited in the following Louisiana studies: Bert and Humm (1979), Humm and Bert (1979), Kapraun (1974), present study
Synonyms from Louisiana studies: as *C. fascicularis* by Mullahy (1959)

Cladophora montagneana Kützing
Taxonomic reference: **Schneider and Searles (1991), Wynne (1986)**
Synonyms from Louisiana studies: as *Cladophora delicatula* Montagne by Humm and Darnell (1959), Bert and Humm (1979), Humm and Bert (1979)

Cladophora sericea (Hudson) Kützing
Taxonomic reference: **Schneider and Searles (1991), Wynne (1986)**
Cited in the following Louisiana studies: Bert and Humm (1979)
Synonyms from Louisiana studies: as *Cladophora gracilis* by Humm and Caylor (1957), Bert and Humm (1979), and Humm and Bert (1979), as *Cladophora flexuosa* (Dillwyn) Harvey by Bert and Humm (1979)

Cladophora socialis Kützing
Taxonomic reference: **Wynne (1986)**, species not included in Schneider and Searles (1991)
Synonyms from Louisiana studies: as *C. constricta* by Bert and Humm (1979)

Cladophora vagabunda (Linnaeus) van den Hoek
Taxonomic reference: **Schneider and Searles (1991), Wynne (1986)**
Cited in the following Louisiana studies: Bert and Humm (1979)
Synonyms from Louisiana studies: as *Cladophora fascicularis* by Humm and Caylor (1957), as *Cladophora brachyclona* Montagne Bert and Humm (1979)

Siphonocladaceae

Cladophoropsis membranacea (C. Agardh) Børgesen
Taxonomic reference: **Wynne (1986)** Cited in the following Louisiana studies: Humm and Darnell (1959), Kapraun (1974), Bert and Humm (1979)
Note: Schneider and Searles (1991) cite two studies from the southeastern states where *Cladophora pellucidoidea* van den Hoek was misidentified as *C. membranacea*.

Rhizoclonium africanum Kützing
Taxonomic reference: **Wynne (1986)**, species not included in Schneider and Searles (1991)
Synonyms from Louisiana studies: as *Rhizoclonium hookeri* by Bert and Humm (1979), Humm and Bert (1979), Kapraun (1974)

Rhizoclonium kochianum Kützing
Taxonomic reference: **Dawes (1974)**, not mentioned by either Schneider and Searles (1991) or Wynne (1986)
Cited in the following Louisiana studies: Humm and Darnell (1959), Bert and Humm (1979), Humm and Bert (1979), Kapraun (1974)

Rhizoclonium riparium (Roth) Harvey
Taxonomic reference: **Schneider and Searles (1991), Wynne (1986)**
Cited in the following Louisiana studies: Humm and Caylor (1957), Bert and Humm (1979), Humm and Bert (1979), Mullahy (1959), Kapraun (1974)
Synonyms from Louisiana studies: as *Rhizoclonium kerneri* by Humm and Bert (1979)

Rhizoclonium tortuosum Kützing
Cited in the following Louisiana studies: Humm and Bert (1979)

Valoniaceae

Valonia macrophysa Kützing
Taxonomic reference: **Wynne (1986)**, not cited by Schneider and Searles (1991)
Cited in the following Louisiana studies: Eiseman and Blair (1982)

Valonia ventricosa J. Agardh
Taxonomic reference: **Wynne (1986)**, not cited by Schneider and Searles (1991)
Cited in the following Louisiana studies: Eiseman and Blair (1982)

Caulerpales
Bryopsidaceae

Bryopsis pennata Lamouroux
    Taxonomic reference: **Schneider and Searles (1991), Wynne (1986)**
    Cited in the following Louisiana studies: Bert and Humm (1979)

Bryopsis plumosa (Hudson) C. Agardh
    Taxonomic reference: **Schneider and Searles (1991), Wynne (1986)**
    Cited in the following Louisiana studies: Kapraun (1974)

Bryopsis hypnoides Lamouroux
    Taxonomic reference: **Wynne (1986)**, species not included in Schneider and Searles (1991)
    Cited in the following Louisiana studies: Bert and Humm (1979)

Derbesia vaucheriaformis (Harvey) J. Agardh
    Taxonomic reference: **Wynne (1986)**
    Cited in the following Louisiana studies: Bert and Humm (1979)
    Note: Schneider and Searles (1991) cite two studies from the southeastern states where *Derbesia marina* (Lyngbye) Solier was misidentified as *D. vaucheriaformis*

Derbesia turbinata Howe and Hoyt
    Taxonomic reference: **Wynne (1986)**
    Cited in the following Louisiana studies: present study

Pedobesia lamourouxii (J. Agardh) J. Feldmann, Loreau, Codomier, and Couté
    Taxonomic reference: **Wynne (1986)**
    Synonyms from Louisiana studies: as *Derbesia lamourouxii* (J. Agardh) Solier by Bert and Humm (1979)
    Note: Schneider and Searles (1991) cite one study from the southeastern states where *Derbesia marina* (Lyngbye) Solier was misidentified as *D. lamourouxii*..

Caulerpaceae

Caulerpa microphysa (Weber van Bosse) Feldman
    Taxonomic reference: **Wynne (1986)**, species not in Schneider and Searles (1991)
    Cited in the following Louisiana studies: Eiseman and Blair (1982)

Caulerpa prolifera (Forskål) Lamouroux
    Taxonomic reference: **Schneider and Searles (1991), Wynne (1986)**
    Cited in the following Louisiana studies: Humm and Darnell (1959), Kapraun (1974)

Caulerpa racemosa var. *laetevirens* (Montagne) Weber-van Bosse
    Taxonomic reference: **Schneider and Searles (1991)**, this variety not in Wynne (1986)
    Cited in the following Louisiana studies: Eiseman and Blair (1982)
    Synonyms from Louisiana studies: as *Caulerpa peltata* by Eiseman and Blair (1982)

Caulerpa racemosa (Forsskål) J. Agardh var. *racemosa*
    Taxonomic reference: **Wynne (1986)**, this variety not in Schneider and Searles (1991)
    Cited in the following Louisiana studies: Eiseman and Blair (1982)

Codiaceae

Codium taylorii (Silva)
    Taxonomic reference: **Schneider and Searles (1991), Wynne (1986)**
    Cited in the following Louisiana studies: Eiseman and Blair (1982)

A-11

Ostreobiaceae

Ostreobium quekettii Bornet and Flahault
    Taxonomic reference: **Schneider and Searles (1991), Wynne (1986)**
    Cited in the following Louisiana studies: Humm and Caylor (1957), Bert and Humm (1979)

Udoteaceae

Halimeda discoidea Decaisne
    Taxonomic reference: **Wynne (1986),** genus not cited by Schneider and Searles (1991)
    Cited in the following Louisiana studies: Eiseman and Blair (1982)

Halimeda gracilis Harvey ex J. Agardh
    Taxonomic reference: **Wynne (1986),** genus not cited by Schneider and Searles (1991)
    Cited in the following Louisiana studies: Eiseman and Blair (1982)

Udotea cyanthiformis Decaisne
    Taxonomic reference: **Schneider and Searles (1991), Wynne (1986)**
    Cited in the following Louisiana studies: Eiseman and Blair (1982)

Udotea flabellum (Ellis and Solander) Lamouroux
    Taxonomic reference: **Schneider and Searles (1991), Wynne (1986)**
    Cited in the following Louisiana studies: Eiseman and Blair (1982)

Dasycladales

Batophora oerstedii J. Agardh
    Taxonomic reference: **Schneider and Searles (1991)**
    Cited in the following Louisiana studies: Bert and Humm (1979)
    Note: Schneider and Searles (1991) cite this species as cast ashore unattached in drift only.

Chrysophyta

Vaucheria velutina C. Agardh
    Taxonomic reference: **Schneider and Searles (1991)**
    Synonyms from Louisiana studies: as *Vaucheria thuretii* Woronin by Humm and Caylor (1957)

Phaeophyta
Phaeophyceae
Ectocarpales
Ectocarpaceae

Acinetospora crinita (Carmichael ex Harvey in Hooker) Kornmann
    Taxonomic reference: **Schneider and Searles (1991), Wynne (1986)**
    Cited in the following Louisiana studies: Bert and Humm (1979)

Bachelotia antillarum (Grunow) Gerloff
    Taxonomic reference: **Schneider and Searles (1991), Wynne (1986)**
    Cited in the following Louisiana studies: Bert and Humm (1979), Humm and Bert (1979), Kapraun (1974), Earle (1969)

Ectocarpus elachistaeformis Heydrich
    Taxonomic reference: after examination **Schneider and Searles (1991)** considered this a valid taxon but Wynne (1986) put it under *Feldmannia elachistaeformis*

A-12

Cited in the following Louisiana studies: Humm and Caylor (1957), Bert and Humm (1979), Humm and Bert (1979), Earle (1969)

Ectocarpus siliculosus (Dillwyn) Lyngbye
Taxonomic reference: **Schneider and Searles (1991), Wynne (1986)**
Cited in the following Louisiana studies: Humm and Caylor (1957), Kapraun (1974), Earle (1969), present study
Synonyms from Louisiana studies: as *Ectocarpus confervoides*, *Ectocarpus dasycarpus* (*E. dasycarpus* only mentioned by Wynne (1986)) by Humm and Caylor (1957), Humm and Bert (1979), Mullahy (1959), Kapraun (1974), Earle (1969)

Ectocarpus variablis Vickers
Taxonomic reference: **Wynne (1986)**
Cited in the following Louisiana studies: Bert and Humm (1979)

Feldmannia irregularis (Kützing) Hamel
Taxonomic reference: **Wynne (1986)**
Synonyms from Louisiana studies: as *Giffordia conifera* by Bert and Humm (1979)

Herponema tortugense (W. Taylor) W. Taylor
Taxonomic reference: **Wynne (1986)**, species not included in Schneider and Searles (1991)
Cited in the following Louisiana studies: Bert and Humm (1979)

Hincksia irregularis (Kützing) Amsler
Taxonomic reference: **Schneider and Searles (1991)**
Synonyms from Louisiana studies: as *Ectocarpus rallsiae* by Humm and Darnell (1959), as *Giffordia rallsiae* in Humm and Bert (1979), Kapraun (1974), Earle (1969)

Hincksia mitchelliae (Harvey) Silva in Silva
Taxonomic reference: **Schneider and Searles (1991)**
Cited in the following Louisiana studies: present study
Synonyms from Louisiana studies: as *Ectocarpus mitchelliae* by Humm and Caylor (1957), Mullahy (1959), as *Giffordia mitchelliae* and *Giffordia indica* (Sonder) Papenfuss and Chihara in Papenfuss by Bert and Humm (1979), Humm and Bert (1979), Earle (1969), Kapraun (1974).
Note: Schneider and Searles (1991) cite studies from the southeast states where *H. mitchelliae* was misidentified as *G. indica*. Although Schneider and Searles (1991) did not synonomize *G. indica* with *H. mitchellieae*, we treat *G. indica* as a synonym of *H. mitchelliae* because 'indica' does not appear to exist as a taxon (is this true?).

Hincksia ovata (Kjellman) P.C. Silva in Silva, Me—ez, and Moe
Taxonomic reference: **Schneider and Searles (1991)**
Synonyms from Louisiana studies: as *Ectocarpus intermedius* by Bert and Humm (1979), Kapraun (1974), Earle (1969)
Note: *E. intermedius* is not treated by either Schneider and Searles (1991) or Wynne (1986) but Schneider and Searles (1991) do cite *Giffordia intermedia* as a synonym of *H. ovata*. In Wynne (1986) as *Giffordia ovata*.

Phaeostroma pusillum Howe and Hoyt
Taxonomic reference: **Schneider and Searles (1991), Wynne (1986)**
Cited in the following Louisiana studies: Bert and Humm (1979), Humm and Bert (1979), Earle (1969)

Spongonema tomentosum valid taxon?
Taxonomic reference: genus and species not in Schneider and Searles (1991), Wynne (1986), or Taylor (1967)
Cited in the following Louisiana studies: Bert and Humm (1979)

Note: see p. 142 in Earle (1969) for description

Streblonema oligosporum Stromfelt
    Taxonomic reference: **Schneider and Searles (1991), Wynne (1986)**
    Cited in the following Louisiana studies: Kapraun (1974)

Chordariales
Chordariaceae

Cladosiphon zosterae (J. Agardh) Kylin
    Taxonomic reference: **Wynne (1986)**, species not in Schneider and Searles (1991)
    Cited in the following Louisiana studies: Kapraun (1974)
    Synonyms from Louisiana studies: as *Eudesme zosterae* (J. Agardh) Kylin by Humm and Darnell
    (1959)

Cladosiphon occidentalis Kylin
    Taxonomic reference:
    Cited in the following Louisiana studies: Earle (1969)

Myrianemataceae

Hecatonema floridanum
    Taxonomic reference: **Schneider and Searles (1991)**
    Cited in the following Louisiana studies: present study

Myrionema orbiculare J. Agardh
    Taxonomic reference: **Wynne (1986),** not cited by Schneider and Searles (1991)
    Synonyms from Louisiana studies: as *Ascocyclus orbicularis* Magnus by Bert and Humm (1979)
    Note: Schneider and Searles (1991) accept the distinction between *Myrionema magnusii* (Sauvageau)
    Lamouroux and *M. orbiculare.*

Myrionema strangulans Greville
    Taxonomic reference: **Schneider and Searles (1991), Wynne (1986)**
    Cited in the following Louisiana studies: Bert and Humm (1979), present study

Sphacelariales
Sphacelariaceae

Sphacelaria rigidula Kützing
    Taxonomic reference: **Schneider and Searles (1991), Wynne (1986)**
    Cited in the following Louisiana studies: present study
    Synonyms from Louisiana studies: as *Sphacelaria furcigera* by Humm and Darnell (1959), Bert and
    Humm (1979), Humm and Bert (1979), Kapraun (1974), Earle (1969)

Sphacelaria tribuloides Meneghini
    Taxonomic reference: **Schneider and Searles (1991), Wynne (1986)**
    Cited in the following Louisiana studies: Humm and Caylor (1957), Bert and Humm (1979), Kapraun
    (1974), Earle (1969)

Dictyotales
Dictyotaceae

Dictyota bartayresii Lamouroux
    Taxonomic reference: **Wynne (1986)**
    Cited in the following Louisiana studies: Eiseman and Blair (1982), Kapraun (1974).

Dictyota cervicornis Kützing
  Taxonomic reference: **Schneider and Searles (1991), Wynne (1986)**
  Cited in the following Louisiana studies: Humm and Caylor (1957), Earle (1969)

Dictyota menstrualis (Hoyt) Schnandter, Hörnig and Weber-Peukert
  Taxonomic reference: **Schneider and Searles (1991), Wynne (1986)**
  Cited in the following Louisiana studies: *Dictyota dichotoma* by Humm and Caylor (1957), Humm and Darnell (1959), Eiseman and Blair (1982), Mullahy (1959), Kapraun (1974), Earle (1969)

Dictyopteris justii Lamouroux
  Taxonomic reference: **Wynne (1986)**
  Cited in the following Louisiana studies: Eiseman and Blair (1982)

Lobophora variegata (Lamouroux) Womersley
  Taxonomic reference: **Wynne (1986)**
  Cited in the following Louisiana studies: Eiseman and Blair (1982), Kapraun (1974)

Padina gymnospora (Kützing) Sonder
  Taxonomic reference: **Schneider and Searles (1991), Wynne (1986)**
  Synonyms from Louisiana studies: as *Padina vickersiae* by Humm and Caylor (1957), Humm and Darnell (1959), Mullahy (1959), Kapraun (1974), Earle (1969)

Padina jamaicensis (Collins) Papenfuss
  Taxonomic reference: **Wynne (1986)**, not in Schneider and Searles (1991)
  Synonyms from Louisiana studies: as *Padina sanctae-crucis* Børgesen by Kapraun (1974)

Spatoglossum schroederi (C. Agardh) Kützing
  Taxonomic reference: **Wynne (1986), Schneider and Searles (1991)**
  Cited in the following Louisiana studies: Eiseman and Blair (1982)

Stypopodium zonale (Lamouroux) Papenfuss
  Taxonomic reference: **Wynne (1986)**, not in Schneider and Searles (1991)
  Cited in the following Louisiana studies: Eiseman and Blair (1982)

Dictyosiphonales
Striariaceae

Hummia onusta (Kützing) Fiore
  Taxonomic reference: **Schneider and Searles (1991), Wynne (1986)**
  Cited in the following Louisiana studies: Bert and Humm (1979), Humm and Bert (1979), Earle (1969)
  Synonyms from Louisiana studies: *Stictyosiphon subsimplex*, *Myriotrichia subcorymbosa* (Holden) Blomquist by Earle (1969)

Myriotrichiaceae

Myriotrichia clavaeformis Harvey
  Taxonomic reference: **Wynne (1986)**, not in Schneider and Searles (1991)
  Synonyms from Louisiana studies: as *Myriotrichia repens* Hauck by Humm and Bert (1979)

Fucales
Cystoseiraceae

Turbinaria tricostata Barton
  Taxonomic reference: **Wynne (1986)**, family not in Schneider and Searles (1991)
  Cited in the following Louisiana studies: Kapraun (1974)—in drift only!

Sargassaceae

Sargassum acinarium (L.) C. Agardh
    Taxonomic reference: **Wynne (1986)**, not in Schneider and Searles (1991)
    Cited in the following Louisiana studies: Kapraun (1974), Earle (1969)

Sargassum filipendula C. Agardh
    Taxonomic reference: **Schneider and Searles (1991), Wynne (1986)**
    Cited in the following Louisiana studies: Humm and Caylor (1957), Mullahy (1959), Kapraun (1974), Earle (1969)

Sargassum fluitans Børgesen
    Taxonomic reference: **Schneider and Searles (1991), Wynne (1986)**
    Cited in the following Louisiana studies: Humm and Caylor (1957), Bert and Humm (1979), Humm and Bert (1979), Kapraun (1974), Earle (1969), present study

Sargassum natans (Linnaeus) Meyen
    Taxonomic reference: **Schneider and Searles (1991), Wynne (1986)**
    Cited in the following Louisiana studies: Humm and Caylor (1957), Bert and Humm (1979), Mullahy (1959), Kapraun (1974), Earle (1969)

Scytosiphonales
Scytosiphonaceae

Rosenvingea intricata (J. Agardh) Børgesen
    Taxonomic reference: **Wynne (1986),** genus but not species cited in Schneider and Searles (1991)
    Cited in the following Louisiana studies: Kapraun (1974)

Rhodophyta
Rhodophyceae
Bangiophycidae
Porphyridiales
Porphyridiaceae

Chroodactylon ornatum (C. Agardh) Basson
    Taxonomic reference: **Schneider and Searles (1991), Wynne (1986)**
    Synonyms from Louisiana studies: as *Asterocytis ramosa* by Bert and Humm (1979)

Stylonema alsidii (Zanardini) Drew
    Taxonomic reference: **Schneider and Searles (1991), Wynne (1986)**
    Synonyms from Louisiana studies: as *Goniotrichum alsidii* by Bert and Humm (1979), Humm and Bert (1979), present study

Compsopogonales
Erythropeltidaceae

Erythrocladia endophloea Howe
    Taxonomic reference: Schneider and Searles (1991), Wynne (1986)
    Synonyms from Louisiana studies: as *Erythrocladia recondita*, *Erythrocladia vagabunda* by Bert and Humm (1979)

Erythrotrichia carnea (Dillwyn) J. Agardh
    Taxonomic reference: **Schneider and Searles (1991), Wynne (1986)**
    Cited in the following Louisiana studies: Bert and Humm (1979), Humm and Bert (1979), Mullahy (1959), Kapraun (1974), present study

Sahlingia subintegra (Rosenvinge) Kornmann
  Taxonomic reference: **Schneider and Searles (1991)**, *Erythrocladia subintegra* not cited by Wynne (1986) although he does list *Erythropeltis subintegra*
  Cited in the following Louisiana studies: present study
  Synonyms from Louisiana studies: as *Erythrocladia subintegra* by Bert and Humm (1979), Kapraun (1974)

Bangiales
Bangiaceae

Bangia autropurpurea (Roth) C. Agardh
  Taxonomic reference: **Schneider and Searles (1991), Wynne (1986)**
  Cited in the following Louisiana studies: Kapraun (1974), Humm and Bert (1979), present study

Florideophycidae
Acrochaetiales
Acrochaetiaceae

Acrochaetium antillarum W. Taylor
  Taxonomic reference: **Wynne (1986)**, not cited by Schneider and Searles (1991) as a species of *Audouinella*
  Cited in the following Louisiana studies: Bert and Humm (1979)

Acrochaetium flexuosum Vickers
  Taxonomic reference: **Wynne (1986)**, not cited by Schneider and Searles (1991) as a species of *Audouinella*
  Cited in the following Louisiana studies: Humm and Darnell (1959), Bert and Humm (1979), Kapraun (1974)

Audouinella densa (Drew) Garbary
  Taxonomic reference: **Schneider and Searles (1991)**
  Cited in the following Louisiana studies: present study

Audouinella gracilis (Børgesen) Garbary
  Taxonomic reference: **Wynne (1986)**, *gracilis* not in Schneider and Searles (1991)
  Synonyms from Louisiana studies: as *Acrochaetium gracile* by Bert and Humm (1979), Humm and Bert (1979)

Audouinella hallandica (Kylin) Woelkerling
  Taxonomic reference: **Schneider and Searles (1991), Wynne (1986)**
  Synonyms from Louisiana studies: as *Acrochaetium dufourii* by Bert and Humm (1979)

Audouinella hoytii (Collins) C.W. Schneider
  Taxonomic reference: **Schneider and Searles (1991), Wynne (1986)**
  Synonyms from Louisiana studies: as *Acrochaetium hoytii* by Bert and Humm (1979)

Audouinella hypneae (Børgesen) Lawson and John
  Taxonomic reference: **Schneider and Searles (1991), Wynne (1986)**
  Synonyms from Louisiana studies: as *Acrochaetium seriatum* by Humm and Caylor (1957), Bert and Humm (1979)

Audouinella microscopica (Nägeli) Woelkerling
  Taxonomic reference: **Schneider and Searles (1991), Wynne (1986)**
  Cited in the following Louisiana studies: present study

Synonyms from Louisiana studies: as *Acrochaetium crassipes* by Humm and Caylor (1957), Mullahy (1959), Kapraun (1974), as *Acrochaetium trifilum* by Bert and Humm (1979)
Note: Schneider and Searles (1991) considered Taylor's (1960) *Kylinia crassipes* to be *Audouinella microscopica*. In addition, Wynne (1986) lists *Audouinella crassipes, Kylinia crassipes*, etc. as synonyms of *A. microscopica*. Neither Schneider and Searles (1991) or Wynne (1986) mention *Acrochaetium crassipes* but, given the above uses of *crassipes*, it seems likely that the Humm and Caylor's (1957) material is *Audouinella microscopica*.

Audouinella sancti-thomae (Børgesen) Garbary
Taxonomic reference: **Wynne (1986)**, not in Schneider and Searles (1991)
Synonyms from Louisiana studies: as *Acrochaetium sancti-thomae* by Bert and Humm (1979)

Audouinella saviana (Meneghini) Woelkerling
Taxonomic reference: **Schneider and Searles (1991)**
Synonyms from Louisiana studies: as *Acrochaetium thurettii* by Bert and Humm (1979), as *Acrochaetium sagraeanum* by Bert and Humm (1979), Humm and Bert (1979)
Note: Schneider and Searles (1991) cite a study where *Audouinella densa* (Drew) Garbary is misidentified as *A. thurettii*.

Audouinella secundata (Lyngbye) Dixon
Taxonomic reference: **Schneider and Searles (1991)**
Synonyms from Louisiana studies: as *Acrochaetium virgatulum* Humm and Bert (1979)

Nemaliales
Galaxauraceae

Galaxaura oblongata (Ellis and Solander) Lamouroux
Taxonomic reference: **Wynne (1986)**
Cited in the following Louisiana studies: Eiseman and Blair (1982)
Synonyms from Louisiana studies: as *Galaxaura cylindrica* (Ellis and Solander) Lamouroux by Eiseman and Blair (1982)

Gelidiales
Gelidiaceae

Gelidium latifolium (Greville) Bornet and Thuret
Taxonomic reference: **Wynne (1986)**
Cited in the following Louisiana studies: present study
Synonyms from Louisiana studies: as *Gelidium corneum* (Hudson) Lamouroux by Humm and Caylor (1957)
Note: Schneider and Searles (1991) do not include *G. latifolium* in the flora of the southeastern states. In addition, Schneider and Searles (1991) cite several studies where *Gellidium pusillum* (Stackhouse) Le Jolis from the southeastern states was misidentified as *G. corneum*.

    Among other characters, material we have collected from platforms is flat and stoloniferous which, if we accept the similarity of the illustration of *G. corneum* in Humm and Caylor (1957) and Wynne (1986) as the taxonomic reference, then our material has to be *G. latifolium*. If we use Schneider and Searles (1991) as a reference, then we must either list *G. corneum* as a valid taxon or identify our material as *Gelidium americanum* (W.R. Taylor) Santelices, which is the closer of the two species listed by Schneider and Searles (1991). Schneider and Searles (1991) do not synonymize *G. corneum*. Also, they have examined no '*G. corneum*' material from the Gulf of Mexico. [Get the paper by Stewart and Norris (1981) on *Gelidium* species from the Gulf of Mexico.]

Gelidium americanum (W.R. Taylor) Santelices
Taxonomic reference: **Schneider and Searles (1991), Wynne (1986)**
Synonyms from Louisiana studies: as *Pterocladia americana* by Bert and Humm (1979)

Corallinales
Corallinaceae

Amphiroa rigida var. *antillana* Børgesen
 Taxonomic reference: **Wynne (1986)**, not in Schneider and Searles (1991)
 Cited in the following Louisiana studies: Eiseman and Blair (1982)

Amphiroa tribulus (Ellis and Solander) Lamouroux
 Taxonomic reference: **Wynne (1986)**
 Cited in the following Louisiana studies: Eiseman and Blair (1982)

Fosliella farinosa (Lamouroux) Howe
 Taxonomic reference: **Schneider and Searles (1991), Wynne (1986)**
 Cited in the following Louisiana studies: Humm and Caylor (1957), Mullahy (1959), Humm and Darnell (1959), Bert and Humm (1979)
 Synonyms from Louisiana studies: as *F. f.* var. *callithamnioides* in Bert and Humm (1979), as *F. f.* var *solmsiana* in Bert and Humm (1979), as *F. atlantica* in Bert and Humm (1979)

Jania adhaerens Lamouroux
 Taxonomic reference: **Schneider and Searles (1991), Wynne (1986)**
 Cited in the following Louisiana studies: Bert and Humm (1979), present study

Jania capillacea Harvey
 Taxonomic reference: **Schneider and Searles (1991), Wynne (1986)** includes *J. capillacea* in *Jania adhaerens*
 Cited in the following Louisiana studies: Humm and Darnell (1959), Kapraun (1974)

Pneophyllum lejolisii (Rosanoff) Chamberlain
 Taxonomic reference: **Schneider and Searles (1991), Wynne (1986)**
 Synonyms from Louisiana studies: as *Fosliella lejolisii* (Rosanoff) Howe by Humm and Caylor (1957), Humm and Darnell (1959), as *Heteroderma lejolisii* by Kapraun (1974)

Lithophyllum pustulatum (Lamouroux) Foslie
 Taxonomic reference: **Campbell and Woelkerling (1990)**
 Synonyms from Louisiana studies: as *Dermatolithon pustulatum* by Kapraun (1974)

Gigartinales
Gymnophloeaceae

Titanophora incrustans (J. Agardh) Feldmann
 Taxonomic reference: **Wynne (1986)**
 Cited in the following Louisiana studies: Eiseman and Blair (1982)

Halymeniaceae

Cryptonemia sp.
 Cited in the following Louisiana studies: Eiseman and Blair (1982)

Grateloupia filicina (Wulfen) C. Agardh
 Taxonomic reference: **Schneider and Searles (1991), Wynne (1986)**
 Cited in the following Louisiana studies: Humm and Caylor (1957), Eiseman and Blair (1982)

Hypneaceae

Hypnea musciformis (Wulfen) Lamouroux
 Taxonomic reference: **Schneider and Searles (1991), Wynne (1986)**

Cited in the following Louisiana studies: Humm and Caylor (1957), Humm and Darnell (1959), Humm and Bert (1979), Mullahy (1959), Kapraun (1974)

Hypnea valentiae (Turner) Montagne
Taxonomic reference: **Schneider and Searles (1991), Wynne (1986)**
Cited in the following Louisiana studies: Kapraun (1974)
Synonyms from Louisiana studies: as *Hypnea cornuta* by Kapraun (1974)

Hypnea pannosa J. Agardh
Taxonomic reference: **Taylor (1967)** lists this taxon as an 'uncertain record'
Cited in the following Louisiana studies: Humm and Darnell (1959), Kapraun (1974)

Kallymeniaceae

Kallymenia westii Ganesan
Taxonomic reference: **Schneider and Searles (1991)**
Cited in the following Louisiana studies: Eiseman and Blair (1982)

Peyssonneliaceae

Peyssonnelia inamoena Pilger
Taxonomic reference: **Schneider and Reading (1987), Wynne (1986)**
Cited in the following Louisiana studies: present study

Peyssonnelia rubra (Greville) J. Agardh
Taxonomic reference: **Wynne (1986)**
Cited in the following Louisiana studies: Eiseman and Blair (1982)
Note: Schneider and Searles (1991) cite several studies from the southeastern states where *Peyssonnelia inamoena* Pilger was misidentified as *P. rubra*.

Peyssonnelia simulans Weber-van Bosse in Børgesen
Taxonomic reference: **Schneider and Searles (1991), Wynne (1986)**
Cited in the following Louisiana studies: Eiseman and Blair (1982)

Phyllophoraceae

Gymnogongrus tenuis J. Agardh
Taxonomic reference: **Wynne (1986)**, species not mentioned by Schneider and Searles (1991)
Cited in the following Louisiana studies: Humm and Caylor (1957)

Solieriaceae

Agardhiella subulata (C. Agardh)
Taxonomic reference: **Schneider and Searles (1991), Wynne (1986)**
Synonyms from Louisiana studies: as *Agardhiella tenera* by Humm and Caylor (1957), Humm and Darnell (1959), Mullahy (1959), as *Solieria tenera* by Kapraun (1974)
Note: *S. tenera* is not synonymized by either Schneider and Searles (1991) or Wynne (1986) but 'tenera' is synonomous with *A. subulata* according to Wynne (1986).

Gracilariales
Gracilariaceae

Gracilaria caudata J. Agardh

Taxonomic reference: **Wynne (1986)**, species not mentioned by Schneider and Searles (1991)
Cited in the following Louisiana studies: Humm and Darnell (1959), Kapraun (1974)

Gracilaria foliifera (Forsskål) Børgesen
Taxonomic reference: **Wynne (1986)**
Cited in the following Louisiana studies: Humm and Caylor (1957), Humm and Darnell (1959), Bert and Humm (1979), Humm and Bert (1979), Mullahy (1959), Kapraun (1974)
Note: Schneider and Searles (1991) cite several studies from the southeast states where *Gracilaria tikvahiae* McLachlan was misidentified as *G. foliifera*.

Gracilaria verrucosa (Hudson) Papenfuss
Taxonomic reference: **Schneider and Searles (1991), Wynne (1986)**
Cited in the following Louisiana studies: Humm and Bert (1979)

Gracilariopsis lemanaeformis (Bory) Dawson, Acleto and Foldvik
Taxonomic reference: **Schneider and Searles (1991)**
Synonyms from Louisiana studies: as *Gracilariopsis sjoestedtii* by Humm and Bert (1979)
Note: as *Gracilaria lemanaeformis* in Wynne (1986)

Rhodymeniales
Rhodymeniaceae

Botryocladia occidentalis (Børgesen) Kylin
Taxonomic reference: **Schneider and Searles (1991)**
Cited in the following Louisiana studies: Eiseman and Blair (1982)

Chrysymenia halymenioides Harvey
Taxonomic reference: **Wynne (1986)**, species not in Schneider and Searles (1991)
Cited in the following Louisiana studies: Eiseman and Blair (1982)

Coelarthrum albertsii (Piccone) Børgesen
Taxonomic reference: **Wynne (1986)**, not in Schneider and Searles (1991)
Cited in the following Louisiana studies: Eiseman and Blair (1982)

Fauchea hassleri Howe and W. Taylor
Taxonomic reference: **Wynne (1986)**, not in Schneider and Searles (1991)
Cited in the following Louisiana studies: Eiseman and Blair (1982)

Ceramiales
Ceramiaceae

Anotrichium tenue (C. Agardh) Nägeli
Taxonomic reference: **Schneider and Searles (1991), Wynne (1986)**
Synonyms from Louisiana studies: as *Griffithsia tenuis* by Humm and Darnell (1959), Kapraun (1974)

Antithamnion cruciatum (C. Agardh) Nägeli
Taxonomic reference: **Schneider and Searles (1991)**
Cited in the following Louisiana studies: Bert and Humm (1979), present study

Antithamnionella elegans
Taxonomic reference: **Schneider and Searles (1991)**
Cited in the following Louisiana studies: present study

Callithamnion sp.
Cited in the following Louisiana studies: present study

Ceramium byssoideum Harvey
    Taxonomic reference: **Schneider and Searles (1991)**, as *Ceramium flacidum* by Wynne (1986)
    Cited in the following Louisiana studies: Humm and Darnell (1959), Bert and Humm (1979), Kapraun (1974)

Ceramium fastigiatum (Roth) Harvey
    Taxonomic reference: **Schneider and Searles (1991), Wynne (1986)**
    Cited in the following Louisiana studies: Humm and Caylor (1957), Bert and Humm (1979), Kapraun (1974)

Ceramium fastigiatum var. *flaccidum* H. Pandersen
    Taxonomic reference: **Wynne (1986), Schneider and Searles (1991)**
    Cited in the following Louisiana studies: as *Ceramium fastigiatum* var. *flaccida* by Bert and Humm (1979)

Ceramium tenuissimum (Roth) Areschoug
    Taxonomic reference: **Wynne (1986)**
    Cited in the following Louisiana studies: Mullahy (1959)
    Note: Schneider and Searles (1991) cite studies from the southeast states where *Ceramium fastigiatum* f. *flaccidum* H. Petersen in Børgesen was misidentified as *C. tenuissimum*.

Compsothamnion thuyoides (J.E. Smith) Schmitz
    Taxonomic reference: **Wynne (1986)**
    Cited in the following Louisiana studies: Eiseman and Blair (1982)

Spyridia filamentosa (Wulfen) Harvey in Hooker
    Taxonomic reference: **Wynne (1986)**
    Cited in the following Louisiana studies: Humm and Caylor (1957), Humm and Darnell (1959), Mullahy (1959), Kapraun (1974)
    Note: Schneider and Searles (1991) cite several studies from the southeast states where *Spyridia hypnoides* (Bory) Papenfuss was misidentified as *S. filamentosa*.

Spermothamnion investiens (P. and H. Crouan in Schramm and Mazé) Vickers
    Taxonomic reference: **Wynne (1986)**
    Cited in the following Louisiana studies: Bert and Humm (1979)
    Note: Schneider and Searles (1991) cite several studies from the southeastern states where *Lejolisia exposita* C.W. Schneider and Searles was misidentified as *S. investiens*.

Dasyaceae

Dasya corymbifera J. Agardh
    Taxonomic reference: **Wynne (1986)**, species not in Schneider and Searles (1991)
    Cited in the following Louisiana studies: Eiseman and Blair (1982)

Dasya baillouviana (S.G. Gmelin) Montagne
    Taxonomic reference: **Schneider and Searles (1991), Wynne (1986)**
    Cited in the following Louisiana studies: Kapraun (1974)
    Synonyms from Louisiana studies: as *Dasya pedicellata* by Mullahy (1959)

Delesseriaceae

Apoglossum ruscifolium (Turner) J. Agardh
    Taxonomic reference: **Schneider and Searles (1991)**
    Cited in the following Louisiana studies: Eiseman and Blair (1982)

Caloglossa leprieurii (Montagne) J. Agardh
    Taxonomic reference: **Schneider and Searles (1991), Wynne (1986)**
    Cited in the following Louisiana studies: Humm and Caylor (1957), Kapraun (1974)

Hypoglossum tenuifolium (Harvey) J. Agardh
    Taxonomic reference: **Schneider and Searles (1991)**
    Cited in the following Louisiana studies: Eiseman and Blair (1982)

Searlesia subtropica (C.W. Schneider) C.W. Schneider and Eiseman
    Taxonomic reference: **Schneider and Searles (1991)**
    Cited in the following Louisiana studies: Eiseman and Blair (1982)

Rhodomelaceae

Bostrichia radicans (Montagne) Montagne
    Taxonomic reference: **Schneider and Searles (1991), Wynne (1986)**
    Cited in the following Louisiana studies: Humm and Caylor (1957), Humm and Bert (1979), Kapraun (1974); includes *f. moniliforme*

Bostrichia tenella (Vahl) J. Agardh
    Taxonomic reference: **Wynne (1986)**, species not in Schneider and Searles (1991)
    Cited in the following Louisiana studies: Humm and Caylor (1957), Humm and Bert (1979)

Chondria collinsiana Howe
    Taxonomic reference: **Wynne (1986)**, species not in Schneider and Searles (1991)
    Cited in the following Louisiana studies: Kapraun (1974)

Chondria dasyphylla (Woodward) C. Agardh
    Taxonomic reference: **Schneider and Searles (1991), Wynne (1986)**
    Cited in the following Louisiana studies: Kapraun (1974)

Chondria leptacremon (Melvill) Dandoni
    Taxonomic reference: **Wynne (1986)**, species not in Schneider and Searles (1991)
    Cited in the following Louisiana studies: Humm and Caylor (1957)

Chondria temuissima (Goodenough and Woodward) C. Agardh
    Taxonomic reference: **Schneider and Searles (1991), Wynne (1986)**
    Cited in the following Louisiana studies: Kapraun (1974)

Digenea simplex (Wulfen) C. Agardh
    Taxonomic reference: **Wynne (1986)**, not mentioned by either Schneider and Searles (1991) or Dawes
    Cited in the following Louisiana studies: Humm and Darnell (1959), Mullahy (1959), Kapraun (1974)

Herposiphonia secunda (C. Agardh) Falkenberg
    Taxonomic reference: **Wynne (1986)**; the latter also recognizes f. *secunda*, f. *tenella* (C. Agardh) Wynne (1986) with *Herposiphonia tenella* (C. Agardh) Nägeli as a synonym of *H. secunda* f. *tenella.*
    Cited in the following Louisiana studies: Humm and Caylor (1957), Bert and Humm (1979)
    Note: Schneider and Searles (1991) have a different treatment of species in this genus and cite several studies from the southeast states where *H. tenella* (not recognized by Wynne (1986)) was misidentified as *H. secunda.*

Laurencia papillosa (C. Agardh) Greville
    Taxonomic reference: **Wynne (1986)**
    Cited in the following Louisiana studies: Bert and Humm (1979)

Laurencia poiteaui (Lamouroux) Howe
> Taxonomic reference: **Schneider and Searles (1991)**, Wynne (1986) recognized *Laurencia poitei* (Lamouroux) Howe but Silva et al. (1987) explained that *L. poitei* is a synonym of *L. poiteaui*. Synonyms from Louisiana studies: as *Laurencia poitei* by Humm and Darnell (1959), Humm and Bert (1979), Kapraun (1974), as *Laurencia gemmifera* Harvey by Mullahy (1959), Kapraun (1974) Note: Schneider and Searles (1991) cite studies suggesting that *L. gemmifera* is conspecific with *L. poiteaui.*

Lophosiphonia cristata Falkenberg
> Taxonomic reference: **Wynne (1986)**, genus not included in Schneider and Searles (1991) Cited in the northern Gulf flora by Bert and Humm (1979)

Lophosiphonia obscura (J. Agardh) Falkenberg in Engler and Prantl
> Taxonomic reference: **Wynne (1986)**, genus not in Schneider and Searles (1991) Synonyms from Louisiana studies: as *L. subadunca* by Bert and Humm (1979), Humm and Bert (1979)

Lophosiphonia sacchoriza Collins and Hervey
> Taxonomic reference: **Dawes (1974)**, species not mentioned by Wynne (1986), genus and species not mentioned by Schneider and Searles (1991) Cited in the following Louisiana studies: Humm and Caylor (1957), Humm and Darnell (1959), Kapraun (1974)

Polysiphonia atlantica Kapraun and Norris
> Taxonomic reference: **Schneider and Searles (1991)** Cited in the following Louisiana studies: present study

Polysiphonia boldii Wynne and Edwards
> Taxonomic reference: **Wynne (1986)** Synonyms from Louisiana studies: as *Polysiphonia hemishperica* by Bert and Humm (1979), Humm and Bert (1979)

Polysiphonia denudata (Dillwyn) Greville ex Harvey
> Taxonomic reference: **Schneider and Searles (1991)** Cited in the following Louisiana studies: Humm and Darnell (1959), Kapraun (1974) Synonyms from Louisiana studies: as *Polysiphonia variegata* by Humm and Caylor (1957), Mullahy (1959)

Polysiphonia echinata Harvey
> Taxonomic reference: **Wynne (1986)**, not in Schneider and Searles (1991) Cited in the following Louisiana studies: Humm and Darnell (1959), Humm and Bert (1979), Kapraun (1974)

Polysiphonia havanensis Harvey
> Taxonomic reference: **Schneider and Searles (1991), Wynne (1986)** Cited in the following Louisiana studies: Humm and Darnell (1959), Bert and Humm (1979), Kapraun (1974)

Polysiphonia howei Hollenberg
> Taxonomic reference: **Schneider and Searles (1991), Wynne (1986)** Cited in the following Louisiana studies: Humm and Caylor (1957), Bert and Humm (1979)

Polysiphonia ramentacea Harvey
> Taxonomic reference: **Wynne (1986)**, species not in Schneider and Searles (1991) Cited in the following Louisiana studies: Mullahy (1959), Kapraun (1974)

Polysiphonia subtilissima Montagne
   Taxonomic reference: **Schneider and Searles (1991), Wynne (1986)**
   Cited in the following Louisiana studies: Humm and Caylor (1957), Bert and Humm (1979), Humm and Bert (1979), Kapraun (1974)

Wrightiella tumanowiezii (Gatty) Schmitz
   Taxonomic reference: **Schneider and Searles (1991), Wynne (1986)**
   Cited in the following Louisiana studies: Humm and Darnell (1959), Kapraun (1974)

Literature Cited in Appendix 1

Bert, T.M. and H.J. Humm. 1979. Checklist of the marine algae on the offshore oil platforms of Louisiana. Rice University Studies 65:437-446.

Campell, S.J. and W.J. Woelkerling. 1990. Are *Titanoderma* and *Lithophyllum* (Corallinaceae, Rhodophyta) distinct genera? *Phycologia* 29:114-125.

Dawes, C.J. 1974. *Marine Algae of the west coast of Florida.* Coral Gables, Florida: University of Miami Press. 201 pp.

Earle, S.A. 1969. Phaeophyta of the eastern Gulf of Mexico. Phycologia 7:71-254.

Edwards, P. 1976. *Illustrated Guide to the Seaweeds and Seagrasses in the Vicinity of Port Aransas, Texas.* University of Texas Press, Austin and London, 128 pp + Addenda.

Eiseman, N.J. and S.M. Blair. 1982. New records and range extensions of deepwater algae from East Flower Garden Bank, Northwestern Gulf of Mexico. *Contr. mar. Sci.* 25:21-26.

Humm, H.J. and T.M. Bert. 1979. The benthic marine algae of Timbalier Bay, Louisiana. *Rice University Studies.* 65:379-399.

Humm, H.J. and R.L. Caylor. 1957. The summer marine flora of Mississippi Sound. *Contr. mar. Sci.*4:228-264.

Humm, H.J. and R.M. Darnell. 1959. A collection of marine algae from the Chandeleur Islands. *Contr. mar. Sci.* 6:265-276.

Kapraun, D.F. 1974. Seasonal periodicity and spatial distribution of benthic marine algae in Louisiana. *Contr. mar. Sci.* 18: 140-167.

Mullahy, J. H. 1959. Preliminary survey of the algal flora of the Chandeleur Islands. *Proc. La Acad. Sci.* 22:62-68.

Schneider, C.W. and R.P. Reading. 1987. A revision of the genus *Peyssonnelia* (Rhodophyta, Cryptonemiales) from North Carolina, including *P. atlantica* new species. *Bull. Mar. Sci.* 40:175-192.

Schneider, C.W. and R.B. Searles. 1991. *Seaweeds of the Southeastern United States: Cape Hatteras to Cape Canaveral.* Durham and London: Duke University Press. 553 pp.

Silva, P.C., E.G. Menez, and R.L. Moe. 1987. Catalog of the benthis marine algae of the Phillipines. Smithsonian Contr. Mar. Sci. 27:i-iv, 179 pp.

Stewart, J. and J.N. Norris. 1981. Gelidiaceae (Rhodophyta) from the northern Gulf of California, Mexico. Phycologia 20:273-284.

Taylor, W.R. 1960. Marine Algae of the eastern Tropical and Subtropical Coasts of the Americas. Ann Arbor: University of Michigan Press. i-ix, 879 pp.

Taylor, W.R. 1967. Marine Algae of the eastern Tropical and Subtropical Coasts of the Americas. 2nd ed. Ann Arbor: University of Michigan Press. i-ix, 870 pp.

Wynne, M.J. 1986. A checklist of benthic marine algae of the tropical and subtropical western Atlantic. Can. J. Bot. 64:2239-2281.

Other relevant literature:

Almodovar, L.R. and D.L. Ballantine. Checklist of benthic marine macroalgae plus additional species records from Puerto Rico. 7-20

Baca, B.J., L.O. Sorensen, and E.R. Cox. 1979. Systematic List of the Seaweeds of south Texas. Contr. Mar. Sci. 22:179-192.

Ballantine, D. and H. Humm. 1975. Benthic algae of the Anclote Estuary I. epiphytes of seagrass leaves. Florida Scientist 38:150-162.

Ballantine, D.L. and M. J. Wynne. 1986. Notes on the marine algae of Puerto Rico.I. additions to the flora. Bot. Mar. 29:131-135.

Ballantine, D.L. and M.J. Wynne. 1986. Notes on the marine algae of Puerto Rico II. Additions of Ceramiaceae (Rhodophyta) including Ceramium vergoniae sp nov. Bot. Mar. 29:497-502.

Bourrelly, P. 1952. Algues d'eau douce de la Guadaloupe et d'ependances: recueillies par la Mission P. Allorge en 1936. Paris: Societe d' Edition d'Enseignment Sup'erieur. 281 pp.

Chapman, V.J. 1961. The Marine Algae of Jamaica: I. Myxophyceae and Chlorophyceae. Bull. Instit. Jamaica 1:3-159.

Chapman, V.J. 1961. The Marine Algae of Jamaica: II. Phaeophyceae and Rhodophyceae. Bull Instit. Jamaica 2:3-201.

Collins, F.S. 1901. The algae of Jamaica. Proc. Amer. Acad. Arts Sci. 37:230-270.

Conover, J.T. 1958. The ecology, seasonal periodicity, and distribution of benthic plants in some Texas lagoons. Bot. Mar. 8:4-41.

Cowper, S.W. 1978. The drift algae community of seagrass beds in Redfish Bay, Texas. Contr. mar. Sci. 21:125-132.

Dawson, E.Y. 1962 Additions to the marine flora of Costa Rica and Nicaragua. Pac. Natur. 3:375-395.

Earle, S. 1972. Benthic algae and seagrasses. In: Chemistry, Primary Productivity, and Benthic Algae of the Gulf of Mexico. Atlas folio no. 22, New York: American Geographical Society. pp. 15-18 and 25-28.

Edwards, P. and D.F. Kapraun. 1973. Benthic marine algal ecology in the Port Aransas, Texas area. Contr. mar. Sci..17:15-52.

Edwards, P. 1969. Field and cultural studies on the seasonal periodicity of growth and reproduction of selected Texas benthic marine algae. Contr. mar. Sci. 14:59-114.

Flint, L.H. 1951. Some winter red algae of Louisiana. Proc. La Acad. Sci. 14:34-36.

Guzman, S.C. 1965. Notas preliminares sobre un reconocimiento de la flora marina del estado de Veracruz. Anal. Instit. Nac. Invest. Biol.-Pesqu. 1:6-49.

Hamm, D. and H. J. Humm. 1976. Benthic algae of the Anclote Estuary II. Bottom-dwelling species. Florida Scientist 39:209-229.

Humm, H. J. 1964. Epiphytes of the sea grass Thalassia testudinum. Florida Bulletin of Marine Science. 14:306-341.

Humm, H. J. and S. E. Taylor. 1961. Marine chlorophyta of the upper west coast of Florida. Bull. Mar. Sci. Gulf and Caribb. 11:321-380.

Humm, H. J. and H. H. Hildebrand. 1964. Marine algae from the Gulf Coast of Texas and Mexico. Contr. mar. Sci. 8:227-268.

Kaldy, J. E., K. H. Dunton, and A. B. Czerny. 1995. Variation in macroalgal species composition and abundance on a rock jetty in the northwest Gulf of Mexico. Bot. Mar. 38:519-527.

Kapraun, D.F. 1970. Field and cultural studies of Ulva and Enteromorpha in the vicinity of Port Aransas, Texas. Contr. Mar. Sci. 15:205-285.

Kapraun, D.F. 1980. Summer aspect of algal zonation on a Texas jetty in relation to wave exposure. Contr. mar. Sci. 23:101-109.

Kapraun, D.F. 1980. An Illustrated Guide to the Benthic Marine Algae of Coastal North Carolina. I. Rhodophyta. Chapel Hill: The University of North Carolina Press. 206 pp.

Kapraun, D.F. 1984. An Illustrated Guide to the Benthic Marine Algae of Coastal North Carolina. II. Chlorophyta and Phaeophyta. Germany: J. Cramer. 173 pp.

Kylin, H. 1956. Die Gattungen der Rhodophycean. Lund, C.W.K. Gleerup, xv, 673 pp.

Lehman, R.L. and J.W. Tunnell, Jr. 1992. Species composition and ecology of the macroalgae of Enmedio Reef, Veracruz, Mexico. Tex. J. Sci. 44:445-457.

Littler, D.S., M.M.Littler, K.E.Bucher, and J.N. Norris. 1989. Marine Plants of the Caribbean: A field guide from Florida to Brazil. Shrewsbury, England: Airlife Publishing Ltd., 263 pp.

Lopez-Bautista, J.M. (unpublished). Lista preliminar de algas marinas bentonicas Tamaulipecas: Arregladas sgun Wynne (1980), excepto Cyanophyta.

Lowe, Jr., G. C. and E. R. Cox. 1978. Species composition and seasonal periodicity of the marine benthic algae of Galveston Island, Texas. Contr. mar. Sci. 21:2-24.

Martinez-Lozano, S. and J. M. Lopez-Bautista. 1991. Algas marinas benticas de soto la marina, Tamaulipas, Mexico. Publ. Biol., F. C. B./U. A. N. L. 5:16-18.

Martinez-Lozano, S. and O. G. Rios. 1991 Lista sistematica de las algas marinas del Puerto El Mezquital, Matamoros, Tamaulipas, Mexico. Biotam 3:16-26.

Martinez-Lozano, S. and L. Villarreal-Rivera. 1991. Algas marinas de San Fernando, Tamaulipas, Mexico. Publ. Biol. F. C. B./U. A. N. L. 5:9-12.

Medlin, L. K. 1984. Short note on changes in the abundance and occurrence of six macroalgal species along the Texas Coast of the Gulf of Mexico. Contr. mar. Sci. 27:85-91.

Pedroche, F. F., K.M. Dreckmann, A.G. Senties, and R. Margain-Hernandez. 1993. Diversidad algal en Mexico. Rev. Soc. Mex. Hist. Nat. XLIV:69-92.

Pedroche, F. F., J. A. West, G.C. Zuccarello, A.G. Senties, and U. Karsten. 1995. Marien red algae of the mangroves in southern Pacific Mexico and Pacific Guatemala. Bot. Mar. 38:111-119.

Phillips, R.C. and V.G. Springer. 1960. Observations on the offshore benthic flora in the Gulf of Mexico off Pinellas County, Florida. Am. Midl. Nat. 64:362-381.

Phillips, R. C. 1960. Ecology and distribution of marine algae found in Tampa Bay, Boca Ciega Bay and at Tarpon Springs, Florida. Q. Jl. Fla. Acad. Sci. 23:222-260.

Phillips, R. C. 1961. Seasonal aspect of the marine algal flora of St. Lucie Inlet and adjacent Indian River, Florida. Q. Jl. Fla. Acad. Sci. 24:135-147.

Phillips, R.C., R.L. Vadas, and N. Ogden. 1982 The marine algae and seagrasses of the Miskito Bank, Nicaragua. Aquat. Bot. 13:187-195.

Schneider, C.W. and R.P. Reading. 1987. A revision of the genus Peyssonnelia (Rhodophyta, Cryptonemiales) from North Carolina including P. atlantica new species. Bull. Mar. Sci. 40:175-192.

Taylor, W.M.R. 1954a. Distribution of Marine Algae in the Gulf of Mexico. Papers Mich. Acad. Sci. Arts Lett. 39:85-109.

Taylor, W.R. 1954b. Sketch of the character of the marine algae vegetation of the shores of the Gulf of Mexico. In: Galtsoff, P. (ed.). The Gulf of Mexico, Its Origins, Waters and Marine Life. Fish Bull. Fish Wildlife Serv. 55:177-192.

Taylor, W.M.R. and A.J. Bernatowicz, 1969. Distribution of Marine Algae about Bermuda. Bermuda Biol. Stat. Res.1:1-42.

Taylor, W.M.R. 1941. Notes on the marine algae of Texas. Papers Mich. Acad. Sci. Arts Lett. 26:69-79.

West, J.A., G.C. Zuccarello, F. F. Pedroche, and U. Karsten. 1994. Caloglossa apomeiotica sp. nov. (Ceramiales, Rhodophyta) from Pacific Mexico. Bot. Mar. 37:381-390.

APPENDIX B

VIDEO PERCENT COVER DATA

ST54 Video Percent Cover (Point Count) 100 points per depth

Depth m.	Bare	Turf	Barnacle	Bacterial Film	Encrusting Sponge (2)	Hydroids	Bryozoans	Algae
1	25	20	43	0	0	5	0	5
1	10	25	39	0	0	8	0	2
1	0	22	24	0	0	12	0	2
1	5	12	28	0	0	12	0	7
1	2	20	40	0	0	4	0	1
1	1	15	38	0	0	9	0	1
2	2	12	41	0	5	15	0	1
3	1	12	37	0	0	21	0	2
4	1	15	38	0	11	37	0	2
5	0	20	30	0	0	50	0	3
5	5	15	30	0	5	50	0	4
5	0	20	10	0	20	50	0	1
5	0	10	60	0	15	25	0	4
5	0	30	25	0	5	10	0	5
6	0	45	10	0	0	20	0	7
7	0	25	20	0	5	40	0	8
8	0	35	30	0	20	10	0	5
9	0	30	25	0	20	30	0	0
10	0	30	17	0	15	45	0	0
10	5	25	13	0	15	45	0	0
10	1	25	15	0	5	54	0	0
10	0	20	27	0	2	53	0	0
10	2	18	46	0	0	35	0	0
11	0	30	26	0	5	40	0	0
12	1	65	11	0	5	19	0	0
13	0	65	10	0	5	18	0	0
14	0	50	20	0	10	10	0	0
15	0	50	21	0	10	10	0	0
16	0	65	36	10	0	0	0	0
17	0	55	36	12	5	5	0	0
18	0	55	36	15	5	5	0	0
19	0	55	36	15	5	5	0	0
20	0	10	60	20	0	10	0	0
20	0	12	50	30	0	8	0	0
20	0	12	50	30	0	8	0	0
20	0	12	50	30	0	8	0	0
20	0	12	50	30	0	8	0	0

GI94 Video Percent Cover (Point Count) 100 points per depth

Depth m.	Bare	Turf	Barnacle	Standing Sponge (1)	Encrusting Sponge (2)	Hydroids	Bryozoans	Tunicates	Bivalves
1	30	0	60	10	0	0	0	0	0
1	10	0	10	80	0	0	0	0	0
1	10	0	10	80	0	0	0	0	0
1	0	0	100	0	0	0	0	0	0
5	0	55	5	30	10	0	0	0	0
5	1	59	15	5	20	0	0	0	0
5	0	33	5	2	50	10	0	0	0
5	0	33	5	0	50	10	0	0	0
6	0	20	0	0	40	40	0	0	0
6	0	40	20	0	30	10	0	0	0
7	0	25	35	0	10	30	0	0	0
8	0	50	0	0	25	20	5	0	0
8	0	55	0	0	10	10	25	0	0
9	0	30	0	0	10	5	55	0	0
10	0	50	0	0	0	50	0	0	0
10	0	45	0	0	0	50	5	0	0
10	0	75	0	0	0	25	0	0	0
10	0	38	0	2	0	20	20	0	0
10	0	40	0	0	0	20	20	0	0
10	0	40	25	0	10	10	15	0	0
11	0	85	0	0	5	5	5	0	0
12	0	73	2	0	5	15	5	0	0
13	0	73	2	0	10	5	0	0	0
14	0	59	1	0	0	10	30	0	0
15	0	23	0	0	2	5	70	0	0
16	0	23	0	0	2	5	70	0	0
17	0	23	0	0	2	5	70	0	0
18	0	10	0	0	5	10	75	0	0
19	0	10	0	0	5	10	75	0	0
20	0	5	0	0	0	50	45	0	0
20	0	20	0	0	75	0	5	0	0
20	0	5	2	0	80	0	13	0	0
20	0	20	0	0	75	0	5	0	0
20	0	5	2	0	80	0	13	0	0
21	0	5	2	0	80	0	13	0	0
22	0	15	0	0	0	0	5	80	0
23	0	15	0	0	0	0	5	80	0
24	0	10	0	0	30	5	5	50	0
25	0	30	0	0	25	5	10	30	0
26	0	50	0	0	30	5	5	0	10
27	0	50	0	0	30	5	5	0	5
28	0	40	0	0	20	40	0	0	0
29	0	50	0	0	20	10	5	10	5
30	0	50	0	0	20	20	10	0	0
30	0	20	0	0	20	10	50	0	0
30	0	20	0	0	20	10	50	0	0
30	0	33	10	0	50	5	2	0	0
30	0	50	5	0	30	5	2	1	0

GC-18 Video Percent Cover (Point Count) 100 points

Depth	Bare	Turf	Barnacle	Standing Sponge	Encrusting Sponge	Hydroids	Bryozoan	Tunicates	Bivalves	Algae	Anemones
1	0	15	5	0	10	15	0	0	0	20	55
1	2	17	8	0	2	12	0	0	0	22	37
1	3	26	8	0	5	12	0	0	0	17	29
1	1	25	15	0	7	13	0	0	0	15	12
1	0	15	2	0	9	6	0	0	0	8	30
2	0	5	1	0	10	2	0	0	0	5	17
3	1	12	2	0	5	21	0	0	0	9	10
4	2	22	5	0	2	21	0	0	0	11	5
5	0	24	0	0	10	30	0	0	0	20	2
5	0	21	5	0	5	24	0	0	0	15	3
5	0	32	7	0	2	22	0	0	0	5	5
5	0	40	10	0	5	25	0	0	0	25	0
5	0	45	8	0	3	12	0	0	0	5	0
6	2	35	7	0	10	15	0	0	2	2	2
7	6	10	25	0	0	30	0	0	0	0	3
8	0	12	10	0	15	18	0	0	1	2	1
8	2	11	12	0	0	45	0	0	0	2	0
9	0	5	20	0	20	65	0	0	0	0	0
10	20	10	15	0	0	0	0	0	5	30	0
10	5	25	15	0	0	35	0	0	10	15	0
10	0	30	10	0	0	60	0	0	0	0	0
10	0	35	5	0	5	40	0	0	0	5	0
10	8	25	4	0	0	60	0	0	0	0	0
11	0	5	2	0	85	10	0	0	0	0	0
12	0	15	7	0	15	20	5	0	2	0	0
13	2	11	15	0	12	50	0	0	0	0	0
14	1	22	5	0	0	35	2	0	0	0	0
15	0	21	15	0	2	27	2	0	1	0	0
16	0	10	12	0	5	27	0	0	0	0	0
17	3	28	5	0	12	51	1	0	0	0	0
18	0	27	20	0	5	47	3	0	0	0	0
19	3	20	17	0	25	53	2	0	0	0	0
20	0	30	10	0	5	60	2	0	0	0	0
20	10	20	15	0	10	45	10	0	0	0	0
20	0	15	0	0	5	80	3	0	0	0	0
20	0	10	5	0	5	80	4	0	0	0	0
20	0	15	20	0	45	20	0	0	0	0	0
21	2	12	5	0	65	10	0	0	0	0	0

The Department of the Interior Mission

As the Nation's principal conservation agency, the Department of the Interior has responsibility for most of our nationally owned public lands and natural resources. This includes fostering sound use of our land and water resources; protecting our fish, wildlife, and biological diversity; preserving the environmental and cultural values of our national parks and historical places; and providing for the enjoyment of life through outdoor recreation. The Department assesses our energy and mineral resources and works to ensure that their development is in the best interests of all our people by encouraging stewardship and citizen participation in their care. The Department also has a major responsibility for American Indian reservation communities and for people who live in island territories under U.S. administration.

The Minerals Management Service Mission

As a bureau of the Department of the Interior, the Minerals Management Service's (MMS) primary responsibilities are to manage the mineral resources located on the Nation's Outer Continental Shelf (OCS), collect revenue from the Federal OCS and onshore Federal and Indian lands, and distribute those revenues.

Moreover, in working to meet its responsibilities, the **Offshore Minerals Management Program** administers the OCS competitive leasing program and oversees the safe and environmentally sound exploration and production of our Nation's offshore natural gas, oil and other mineral resources. The MMS **Minerals Revenue Management** meets its responsibilities by ensuring the efficient, timely and accurate collection and disbursement of revenue from mineral leasing and production due to Indian tribes and allottees, States and the U.S. Treasury.

The MMS strives to fulfill its responsibilities through the general guiding principles of: (1) being responsive to the public's concerns and interests by maintaining a dialogue with all potentially affected parties and (2) carrying out its programs with an emphasis on working to enhance the quality of life for all Americans by lending MMS assistance and expertise to economic development and environmental protection.

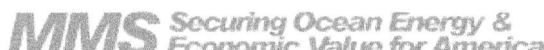